Roads Once Traveled
(In the hills of the Blue Ridge)

By H Wayne Easter

"Roads Once Traveled" continues from my first book, "In the Foothills of Home." It was about my family, my grandparents, and how we lived, worked, and played during the Great Depression. "Roads" is about the friends, neighbors, and kin people who lived along a half-dozen roads in same area, and how *they* lived, worked, and played.

Contents

Preface

Our country roads were a little off the beaten track: unpaved, ankle-deep dusty in summer, and knee-deep muddy in winter. Anyone who drove on them became an expert at fixing flat tires and pushing cars out of the mud. When my dad bought our first car; we too became experts covered with mud.

Like most of our neighbors, we lived on a one-horse farm; plowed the land, sowed the seeds, and swore by the almanac. The seasons ruled our lives and anyone who didn't follow moon signs was "some kinda' furriner' with no red dirt in his blood."

Our neighbors were our friends, with whom we swapped barn-raisings, corn shuckings and weather forecasts. We traveled the highways of life in the same leaky boat and rowed with the same broken paddle. We kept a close an eye on each other, and when a stranger came through, we kept *both* eyes on *him*.

Found in the following pages are some thoughts and memories of people I grew up with in the backwoods of yesterday. Almost all lived within a five-mile area along a half-dozen roads in the Pine Ridge, Round Peak, and Lambsburg areas: a dozen miles west of Mt Airy, North Carolina.

My story begins and ends on Stewart's Creek, and includes photos of some of the people I knew best, along with crude maps, drawings, and photos of their homes and buildings as they stand today: original, dilapidated, re-modeled or replaced. Many of the buildings, like almost all of the owners, have been gone for a very long time.

I apologize in advance for anyone or anything not included, and trust you will forgive my mistakes and mutilations of the English language.

Chapter 1
Road to the Neighborhood

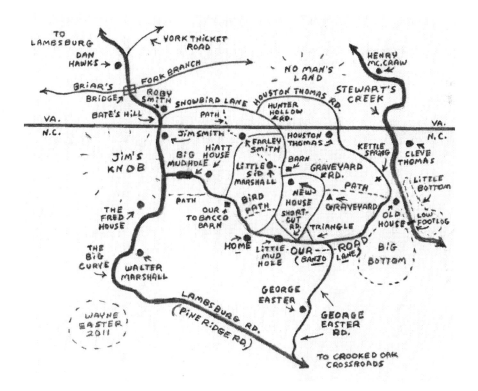

The Neighborhood

Road to the Neighborhood

Our home on Banjo Lane

Often no more than a wagon track or a wide cow path, a road of some sort led to every home in the neighborhood. Our road was one of those and had no name; we called it simply, "Our Road." It was a highway in summer, but in winter, to tell it in our native dialect, "They won't nobody goin' nowhere at no time, never" (With no automobile, we hadn't planned on going anywhere much anyway.)

Our road branched off Lambsburg Road at the foot of Jim's Knob, led through the Big Mud Hole, past the Hiatt House and continued to our house a half-mile down the hill. We lived at the bottom of the barrel in what began as a one-room log cabin my parents built in 1936.

Modern had not yet been invented down our way, and having no choice in the matter, we literally dug a living from the rocky hillsides. As did our neighbors, we dodged every disaster that came our way, and almost eked out a living.

Our neighbors were scattered, but thanks to the grapevine, news traveled faster than the speed of light. In the blink of an eye, no matter where they lived, the news got around, sometimes before it happened.

Our road continued by our house to what we called the Triangle: where three roads came together. Both the Graveyard and Shortcut Roads led to Oscar Marshall's "New House" in the valley: one of the finer homes in our area.

Fisher's Peak, as seen from the Triangle (1971)

Fisher's Peak could be seen from the Triangle area and since most of our weather came from that direction, I kept an eye on it. When rain or snow came over the top, I could almost without fail, predict weather in the immediate future.

Our unfenced garden was near the Triangle, and as my dad said it, "Every horse and cow in the whole d… country eats us outta' house n' home." When a stray animal came calling, he cured its hunger with his shotgun and sent it, again as he told it, "High-tailing it back over the road to wherever the H… it came from.

The George Easter Road

Two hundred feet beyond the Triangle, the George Easter Road forked right to my grandparent's home in the valley. They too had no modern conveniences, but with a horse, a few simple tools, baling wire and twine, they too held everything together. When a big snow came over the mountain, Grandpa scraped our road with his horse and homemade snowplow.

The Old House

Our road continued a half-mile downhill to a one-room log cabin on the banks of Stewart's Creek: built by John Coalson around 1880. Log cabins were said to last a hundred years and the "Old House" (as it was known) almost made it. Over a period of many years, many different families lived there and called it home.

The white oak roof shingles were curled up due to being made in the wrong moon sign, and the spaces between the logs were daubed with red mud: most of which had fallen out. The front doorstep was a large creek rock and several more supported the four house corners. The eave boards were dark brown from long exposure to the weather.

Some older cabins had no windows: only a hole in the wall with a shutter (a wooden cover) that could be closed in bad weather, like at Jim Smith's house. The very oldest cabins, like my grandfather's first house, had nothing but a door and it was dark inside, even in the middle of the day.

The Old House was a little more up-to-date: with a window that looked out on Stewart's Creek, Oscar's two bottoms, the "biggest pine tree in the country" and the Cleve Thomas Woods beyond Stewart's Creek.

The rough-plank front door was held together with a z-brace, and someone had shot a hole in it with a shotgun when John Coalson lived there. (When a Lambsburg man tried to corner the liquor-making market, John refused to work for him, and some of his men came on horseback and shot John through the front door. It wasn't fatal and he heard one of them say that he might still be alive and maybe they should shoot some more. They didn't, and John lived to be an old man.)

The inside walls were covered with newspapers, glued there with flour paste to block the winter wind. Even so, it was "a little airish" inside, but thanks to a roaring fireplace and a stack of quilts to wrop' up in, it was possible to stay alive.

Oscar and Lillie Marshall eventually bought the cabin and the 95 acres of land, and lived there for a time. After they moved away, they called the cabin "The Old House at the Old Place."

Sam Coalson lived there alone in the late 1930s, and looked about as old as the house. He moved slowly, wore overalls, an overall jacket, had white hair, a bushy white beard, and looked a lot like Santa Clause.

He cooked corn bread in a black iron skillet in the rock and mud fireplace, while I read his news-papered walls. He said he could look through the shotgun hole and see who was out there. I was almost afraid to look, because somebody might shoot again, right through the same hole: right into my eye.

I never knew why Pa built our house on a hilltop, so far from the spring. Maybe it was because he didn't have to carry the water. If I ever built a house, my spring would be above the house just like Sam Coalson's. Since his spring was uphill in the pasture, he carried water *downhill* instead of *uphill,* as we did. While carrying two buckets at a time, my tongue dragged on the ground, just like the buckets. (Two buckets took half as many trips.)

An old well in the front yard was never used, but that would've been even easier than carrying water downhill. It was covered with rotten planks and we were told to "stay the heck out of there."

We sharecropped Oscar's bottoms in the early years, along with three others on Stewart's Creek. Fact of the matter, we grew corn anywhere Pa found a field made of dirt. We plowed, planted, hoed, pulled fodder, cut tops and sweated all spring, summer and fall. In late fall, we hauled un-ending wagonloads of corn back home on my grandfather's wagon.

An old nearby barn had a tin roof, no door and no chinking between the logs. We were told, "You young'uns stay outta' there, cause they's copperheads, rattlesnakes, blue-tailed scorpions, black widders', and no telling what else in there." (Apparently, danger lurked around every bend in the road: just waiting to wipe us kids off the face of the Earth, and we would be lucky devils if we saw the sun rise tomorrow.)

It was said when a horse or mule stayed inside a log barn too long, it became a crack-runner, and spent all of its daylight hours pacing back and forth looking out through the cracks. With no chinking between the logs, Oscar's barn was the type of place that could happen. With so many dangerous varmints inside, I "stayed the heck out of there." No way would I ever be a crack runner.

The Lower Hole

My favorite fishing hole on all of Stewart's Creek was beside Oscar's Big Bottom: we called it the "Lower Hole." It was a great place to doze and laze on hot summer days, whether the fish bit or not.

I sat in the shade of alder bushes, dreamed up some great missions, and watched walnuts grow on a tree on the far bank. All the while, Stewart's Creek rolled by on its way to an ocean, "way down yonder somewhere. (I planned to follow it all the way down, someday, but never got around to it.)

The Lower Hole fed into the Swimming Hole: where skinny dippers dived from a huge rock. Pa and I did some big-time diving on hot summer days, but we never learned to swim.

The "biggest white pine in the country" stood on the hill above the Swimming Hole and could be seen, as Pa said it, "from everywhere n' half a' Georgia." Robert Earl East later sawed it down, and according to Mama, "Pa couldn't find his way home."

An old roadway led by the barn, through the middle of Oscar's Big Bottom to a ford that crossed the creek beside the Low Foot Log. In earlier years, it continued through the middle of the Little Bottom on the other side, then uphill through the Cleve Thomas Woods to his house, but now ended at the creek.

In the years we sharecropped the Little Bottom, we hauled bags of fertilizer across the creek on Grandpa's wagon, because our sled went under water. In late fall, we hauled wagonloads of corn back across the ford.

The Low Foot Log was a round un-hewed log that had a mind of its own and it didn't like people. When you got out in the middle, it bounced like a rubber ball, but with a good sense of balance, it was possible to get across the creek without drowning.

Some un-steady on their feet souls took some un-wanted baths when they fell in: sometimes their only bath of the year. Those you could smell a mile away and if you met one on a dark road at midnight, nobody had to tell you who it was: you knew him sight-un-seen. Rumor had it that one of our neighbors lost five pounds when he fell in and all the dirt washed off.

Come November and December, we broke ivy in the Cleve Thomas Woods and carried the full sacks back across the Low Foot Log. Knowing how cold the water was gave me a great sense of balance.

Just downstream, a stretch of roaring rapids splashed over knee-high rocks into the Lower Hole. When the air was just right, we could hear them from our house far in the night: singing me a fishing song.

A high hill to the west was a lifesaver when hoeing corn in the Big Bottom, because it caused the sun to go down earlier. When working the high ridges, it almost never went down and I could almost swear it stood still in the sky, just like it did in the bible. On some of the hottest day, I don't think it ever went down.

One late August day, we pulled fodder in the Big Bottom, as whippoorwills flew around overhead in every direction: headed south for the winter. After watching them a while, I figured they had no idea where south was, or how to get there.

7

The old folks said, "They comes a cool spell ever' August that ends Dog Days." I'd had very little experience along those lines, but I knew for a fact, it had been one heck of a hot summer.

We took a break in the shade, and while lying back in the cool grass, I could almost breathe again in the cool air. For the first time ever, I knew for sure: Dog Days had already gone back down-south where they belonged and we'd almost survived the "hottest summer I ever seen."

Our road ran close to the Old House, continued down the knoll, crossed the spring branch and led up-stream toward the hill-top home of Houston Thomas. The road had been dug out of the hillside long ago, and according to my parents, it was once well used. Except for people on foot and an occasional horse or mule rider, there was almost no traffic in my time. (When all the county roads were named in later years, our road became Banjo Lane.)

Our road continued upstream by the Upper Hole: the only place where I could fish from the road. It then led into the woods by the Kettle Spring, where someone had installed an enamel kettle for a water basin. All who came by drank "that special Kettle Spring Water," and like every other spring in the country, it had the "coldest water in the country."

The road continued uphill by the Houston Thomas house, crossed the State line and continued through the edge of No Man's land to Lambsburg Road in Virginia.

Back at the Old House, a no longer used garden space had grown up in weeds, blackberry briars, locust and sassafras bushes, wild strawberries, and red plums. (Knowing how to find wild food was a matter of survival when running backwoods missions.)

A footpath led uphill through an old pasture overgrown with small pines. Looking back downhill, the Old House looked like it was sitting in the bottom of a big bowl and I could almost see down the chimney.

The footpath continued to the Graveyard Road on top of the hill and a small cemetery, where some of the people who once lived in the Old House were buried. Included were two each of John Coalson and Fred Marshall's children. The flat "sand- rock" headstones had no names or dates and by the 1940s, tall trees had already grown up among the graves. (Following tradition, the people were buried with their heads to the west: assuring sunshine in their faces when they rise up on resurrection morning.)

(In 2011, I made a trip back to the graveyard: my first since the 1940s. I finally found it when I stumbled into the single strand of barbed wire Verlon Marshall had strung around the graves many years ago. The area was overgrown in an ivy thicket and the barbed wire was in the middle of the trees he had nailed it to. The head stones were very weatherworn, and I only found four.)

The barbed wire at the graveyard (2011)

Verlon Marshall's graveyard sign (2011)

Turning *left* on the Graveyard Road led through a stand of tall white pines, and back to the Triangle on our road. Turning *right,* led by our house and on to Lambsburg Road, while turning *left* led back to the Old House on Stewart's Creek.

Back at the path from the Old House, turning *right* on the Graveyard Road led downhill through some de-timbered woods to Oscar Marshall's New House in the valley. We lived there in 1936, while our new log house was being built up on the hill.

The New House

Lillie and Oscar Marshall and family. (1930s)
From the left in back: Lillie, Oscar, Alec and James.
From the left in front: Betty Jo, Gertrude, and Benton (Photo courtesy of Judy Marshall Fulda)

The New House had walls of unpainted wood siding: several rooms and a front porch mounted on posts. Oscar said he could dip water from the spring with a long-handled gourd and never leave the kitchen. (I hardly knew the family in the early years, because they had moved to Lambsburg.)

As time passed, different families lived there for short periods of time, but the house mostly stood empty and my brother Warren and I often went back to play. While climbing alone in the barn loft one day, I slipped, fell, and landed downstairs with my belly across the wall of the feed bin. I wheezed for a very long time and thought I would never breathe again.

The New House spring branch idled along beside a laurel bluff and joined a larger branch formed by the spring branches of Little Sid Marshall, Jim and Farley Smith, who lived back up the valley. The combined branches continued by Little Sid's broom-straw field, through a wooded area and fell into Stewart's Creek beside the Upper Hole.

Little Sid Marshall's home

Oscar's brother Little Sid lived beyond the branch in a log cabin halfway up the hillside in a broom straw field. The house had a frame kitchen on the back, a front porch, a roof made of white oak shingles, and an apple tree grew in the front yard.

Sid did almost no farming in my time, but helped neighbors and kinfolks on their farms. I figured he was far ahead of the game, because farming required big animals that had to be fed every day and they could put away a bunch of feed, which somebody had to grow.

11

After a few days of hoeing corn in the hot summer sun, I *knew for a fact*: Little Sid Marshall was a smart man. His son Emmitt was no dummy either when he grew up. Pa said, "Emmitt can make money settin' on a rock.")

Little Sid and Emmitt in the late 1920s
(Courtesy of Helen Haunn.)

Emmit's mom died when he was born in 1927 and since Little Sid did all the cooking, he enjoyed eating away from home. He ate at our house on occasion and sometimes ate with my grandparents. Grandma once gave him some cake that had fallen apart, and when she apologized for the scrambled cake, Sid said that was the way he liked cake.

He only wore a necktie once in his whole life and as he told it, "I tried it one time and had a hard time gittin' it on and an even harder time gittin' it off. Hadn't been for my pocket knife, that dad blamed thing would'a choked me to death." Little Sid died in 1968, some 40 years after his wife, and Emmett died in 2002.

Little Sid's spring was in the woods across the valley: about as far from home as ours, and they too carried water uphill. When Emmitt built his own home in later years, he installed a "Buttin' (Butting) Ram" in the spring: a mechanical device that used the force of moving water to power it. The contraption made a clack-clack noise every few seconds, as it pumped water up to the house. It worked well until it became clogged with leaves and trash, but whatever problems it had, it beat the heck out of carrying water up-hill in a bucket.

My storybook heroes camped outdoors in all kinds of weather: blizzards, thunderstorms, hail and the dark of night. Except for thunderstorms and the dark of night, I too was outside in all kinds of weather and sometimes camped.

The big difference: *my* trips were made in the daytime and with Fisher's Peak and Sugar Loaf Mountains hanging in the sky, no way could I get lost; I always knew the way home, especially at suppertime. (I did wonder if they got as cold as I did while mushing a deep snow.)

One hot summer day, I hiked in to Little Sid's spring and built a campfire. The great outdoorsman burned some of Mama's wheat bread on a stick, fried some fatback and boiled coffee in a tin can: just like they did it in the Great North Woods.

I learned right away that hot coffee on a hot day was warm, to say the least: especially when trying to drink it from the hot tin can it was just boiled in. I wondered if my heroes ever got smoke in their eyes and sweated over their campfires. According to what I'd read, they were so tough; they drank coffee "straight off the fire," then lit their pipes by breathing on the tobacco.

A footpath led uphill from Little Sid's to Farley and Cleo Smith's home in Hoot Owl Holler'. It passed by their garden: one of the best around: where everything they planted headed for the sky.

Their pasture was just beyond, and just like ours, it was well grazed and the best grass grew two feet outside the fence. All animals knew the grass was greener on the other side of the fence and worked hard to reach it. For that reason, barbed wire was stapled on the inside of the posts to keep the animals from pushing the staples out. "Put your 'bob wire on the outside boy, and they'll push 'er plumb into the next county, by crackity."

The Smith's road ran beside the pasture to their log home in a small valley. It had a frame kitchen at back, an upstairs loft and a wood shingle roof. The front door step was a large field rock and spaces between the logs were daubed with red mud. There was no underpinning and a window in the south end looked out on a spring branch that came from up the valley.

The inside walls of most log homes were covered with newspaper and magazine pages: glued there with flour paste to block the winter wind. The Smith's walls were like a library, and I read them every time I stopped by. One story I've never forgotten was about a man with red airplane he and his dog flew into the wild blue yonder. From high in the sky, they could see the tiny roads and homes on the green Earth. (Why I couldn't I have been his dog for just one day?)

The Farley and Cleo Smith home

The Smith kids were Rufus, Myrtle, Mabel, Edna, and Willie. All were well mannered, and were never threatened with bodily harm, as was done at our house. Rufus and I stayed all night with Pa, when he cured tobacco in my grandfather's barns. We roasted potatoes and apples in the barn flues and slept in the pack house in the wee hours: using old dusty tobacco sacks for cover.

We planned to get rich by selling hand-whittled baseball bats and roasted peanuts. We finally got two poles nailed together for a store building, the first bat was never finished; we ate all the peanuts, and never made the first dime.

Like every other woman on Stewart's Creek, Cleo was a hard worker: with the health and welfare of her children coming before anything else. She scrubbed clothes on a washboard in a big black wash pot, made lye soap, and canned food for winter: all in the same pot.

Farley died when I was young and an all night wake was held at home. He was the first person I'd seen that had died, and he was lying in the open casket with coins over his eyes, as was the custom. It was a scary time and I didn't quite understand what had happened. (Cleo later married John Hawks and they moved away from Hoot Owl Holler.')

Cleo Smith

Another road from the Smith's home led across a log-floored bridge over the spring branch. A path on the left led back to Little Sid's spring: where a certain campfire got drowned with sweat. The road continued uphill beside Jim Smith's pasture and joined "our road" where our tobacco barn would be built in later years.

Another path led west from their house, passed their "bold" spring in the woods, and continued through a pasture to Roby Smith's home on Bates hill. I once found a cow skull in the pasture, but nobody knew where it came from. (A dead cow could be a serious problem for somebody who liked milk as well as I did.)

The footpath continued to Snowbird Lane, where turning right led back to Farley and Little Sid's homes on Hunter Hollow Road. Another road led over a hill to the Houston Thomas place far away on Stewart's Creek. It was a very long road through the edge of No Man's Land: the only way an automobile could get to Houston's house.

15

Turning *left* on Snowbird Lane led to Bates Hill: just north of the North Carolina/Virginia state line. In the early 1900s, John Bates and his wife built a log cabin on the hill and moved there from the Tom's Creek area of Pilot Mountain. Two of their four children died there and were buried in a field east of the house. They then sold the place to Wesley Lyons and moved back to Tom's Creek.

Grady Hawks later bought the house, sat on the front porch in late evenings and played his claw-hammer banjo for the whole world to hear. Bates Hill then had a second name: "Banjo Hill," and everybody knew it by both names.

The John Bates/Roby Smith home on Bates/Banjo Hill

Around 1920, Roby and Sarah Smith built the "Hiatt House" on our road, and lived there until the mid 1920s, when they bought the John Bates place. Their kids were Hurley, Hazel, Clarence, Glenn, Claude, Crissie, and Florence.

Roby was a tall slim man who snapped his fingers and hummed as he walked along. Like most of our neighbors, he never owned a car, which may have been why he and Little Sid Marshall smiled all the time. Some people who owned one got mad and stayed that way when it quit running, or got stuck in a mud hole.

A spring path led downhill from Roby's house, crossed Lambsburg Road and continued to their spring at the Foot of Jim's

16

Knob. Sawmill workers and bootleggers (the only people who had money) met there on weekends, and played poker on the big tree roots that grew in the path. (Few people in our world had enough money to buy what they really needed, let alone enough to play poker.)

Roby Smith in 1966
(Courtesy of Rachel Senter Smith)

Jim's Knob Lane (built in 1962) at the top of Bate's Hill.

Lambsburg Road continued to the top of Bate's Hill, crossed the North Carolina/Virginia state line, and continued southeast to Crooked Oak Crossroads and Pine Ridge. The Virginia part eventually became Chestnut Grove Road and when Surry County named all the county roads, the North Carolina part became Pine Ridge Road.

Foxhunters parked their pickups at the state line on Saturday nights, built a campfire, and listened to their dogs run in the knobs. On Sundays, locals met there, played poker, shot the breeze, told tall tales and drank moonshine from fruit jars. In earlier times a teenage boy was shot and killed at "The Line" during an argument.

Jim and Carrie Smith's home and wine barn

Jim and Carrie Smith lived in a two-room log cabin just south of the state line. They had no driveway and visitors parked their cars halfway in the road, as Boyd McKinney did one day in the 1940s. He had just returned home after losing a leg in the Big War, and his new car had special attachments to help him drive. I'd never seen or smelled a new car before and it had no mud on it.

The house was covered with white oak shingles and had no windows: just holes in the walls: with wooden covers (called shutters) that could be opened or closed according to the weather. That allowed air and light inside, but also allowed flies, mosquitoes, and other flying varmints. Just like at our house, fly swatters and pull-down sticky flycatchers stayed on standby all summer.

18

The doors were made of rough-planks: with latchstrings hanging outside to open them with, and wooden buttons inside to secure them at night. (When the latchstrings were pulled back inside, the welcome mat was no longer out.)

The combination living room/bedroom was heated with a rock-and-mud-fireplace and except for the cook stove in the kitchen; it was their only source of heat. Both the front door step and the fireplace hearth were huge flat rocks and a good luck horseshoe hung over the front door: with the ends pointed up to catch any luck that came by.

Jim's wooden toolbox sat just inside the front door and was crammed with strange wonders. The highlight of my day was playing with the tools and according to Mama; no other kids were allowed to do that. The most amazing thing was a monkey wrench that adjusted to fit all sizes of bolts. Pa and Grandpa had a couple of small wrenches to replace plow points and tighten plow-handles, but none were adjustable.

In the late 1930s, people came from all over on Saturday nights to listen to the Grand 'Ole Opry on the Smith's battery-powered radio. It was the first in our area, and everybody came to hear Uncle Dave Macon, Roy Acuff, and Lonnie Glosson on the *"Grandpa Opry"* program from Nashville, Tennessee. When the batteries ran down, there was no more radio until new ones came in the mail.

It was said the radio signals came in through the air and were picked up by an "earl" wire tied to an apple tree outside. I wondered how they got up there in the first place and kept a close watch, but never saw anything going up or coming down.

Jim was a tall man who wore overalls and an overall jacket, smiled all the time and moved " a little slow." (Since he was getting on in years, he may have been moving as fast as he could.) Carrie was "sickly" and Mama baked cornbread for them and did other chores.

Their children had been gone from home for many years, and the only two I knew at that time were their sons Farley and Roby, who were our neighbors. On cold winter days, Jim and Carrie sat by the fireplace and watched the world go by in the flames.

Carrie's pride and joy was her front yard flower garden, where she grew a dozen kinds of flowers, including something called catnip. A low-growing plant called "house leak" grew under the roof drip-line at back and tiger lilies grew beside the path to the wine barn. Even after she could no longer walk well, Carrie tended her flower and vegetable gardens on her knees.

Jim and Carrie Smith: about 1938

The Smith's spring was downhill in the woods, and they carried water uphill like we did. Persimmon trees grew along the pasture fence and Jim told me, "Boy, when you see a 'possum eatin' them 'simmons, you'll know they're ripe and it ain't gonna' happen 'til it frosts." One pre-frost taste test proved that theory beyond all doubt. Five pounds of sugar would not have cured anything that bitter.

Their low-slung cowshed was just like my grandfather's: old, made of small logs, with a plank roof and almost tall enough for the cow to get inside. At best, it may have kept her dry in a light drizzle.

A path led through a sprout patch to their son Farley's house in Hoot Owl Holler'. Sprout patches came into being when all the trees were cut from an area, and when the stumps, roots, and rocks were dug out, they became new fields. It was extremely hard work and like Grandpa, Jim was getting on in years and didn't need any more new fields. "If you want'a kill them sprouts, boy, chop 'em down in the dark nights of August."

Jim no longer farmed, but grew peanuts and made wine when I was growing up. He no longer climbed ladders, and didn't care who ate the great cherries on his trees.

We sharecropped his field on the side of Nettle's Knob, which my family called "Jim's Knob." Jim's grandson Hurley Smith said he'd never heard the name until my family began calling it that.

(While in the army in 1954, I wrote my brother Warren a letter from Fort Lewis and told him when I got back home, I was going to dig myself a cave on Jim's Knob. Mama still has the letter. In 1955, my armored outfit parked some self-propelled guns on a snowy German hillside that looked exactly like Carrie's garden and Jim's Knob. At that time, we were living in tents in the snow, and I desperately needed to be back home on Jim's Knob.)

The wine barn (2002)

Jim had rows and rows of grapes and didn't care how many I ate. All were out-of-this-world-good except some small blue devils that grew on the wall of the wine barn; they were so sour nobody could eat them.

He stored wine in the barn, and people came from all over and bought it for 25 cents per pint, along with his roasted peanuts for five cents per bag. (His 'bought" peanuts were twice as good as the free peanuts we had at home.) One older lady, who could no longer chew well, tied peanuts in a piece of cloth, pulverized them with a hammer, then ate them.

The Wine Barn was built of chestnut logs before blight killed all of the chestnut trees in the 1920s. Pieces of bark remained on the logs and the spaces between them were chinked with split logs. The pine plank eave boards had turned dark reddish brown from long exposure to the weather.

Jim's wine barn in the 1940s: l to r: Porter and Francis Bryant and Aaron Brintle, grandchildren of Jim and Carrie Smith.

Carrie died in 1945, and Jim moved away to live with his daughter Addie and her husband Watt Bryant on Bryant Road. Pa bought Jim and Carrie's farm at auction, and we then owned part of one of my favorite places in the whole world: Jim's Knob.

(In 1962, Helen and I bought ten acres of land from Frank Coalson and we then owned the very top of Jim's Knob. We made plans to build a house there, but after a very snowy winter, we changed our minds about moving "back to the land.")

When my dad died in 1984, Mama sold the home place on Banjo Lane, and bought back an acre of the Jim Smith land they had previously sold to Crissie Smith. She bought a new house trailer and set up house keeping beside the wine barn.

She had a stroke in 2005, was confined to a rest home for a few weeks, then checked herself out and returned home. As of today, (2011) she is 95, and except for some daytime help from a health care lady, she still lives alone. She says, "I ain't going back to no rest home."

Mama's new home beside the wine barn (1985)

(Footnote: Mama died January 16, 2013 at age 96.)

At the North Carolina/Virginia state line on
Lambsburg (Pine Ridge) Road

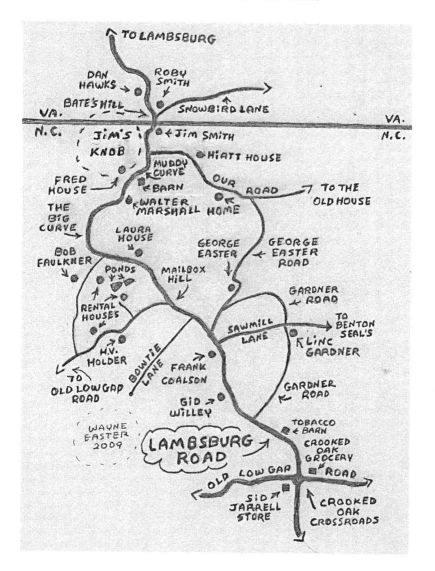

Road to the Crossroads

Our main public road began in Lambsburg, Virginia, crossed the state line and continued to the seat of Surry County in Dobson N C. It was once known as Dobson Road, but we called it "Lambsburg Road." The Virginia section eventually became Chestnut Grove Road, and the North Carolina section became Pine Ridge Road.

Lambsburg Road was a muddy nightmare in winter, and every car that came by got stuck in the mud: buried completely to the axles, and anyone who tried to push it out got buried to the knees. On road-working day, neighborhood men gathered mattocks, shovels, drag-pans, mules and manpower, and tried to repair the worst places. No matter hard they tried, Lambsburg Road remained the "worst road in the country." (When the state finally assumed upkeep, the only difference: the mud was then mixed with gravel.)

One day in the late 1930s, I watched my dad and others work on Walter Marshall's Curve at the foot of Jim's Knob. The curve was said to be, "the worst place in the worst road in the whole country."

It was so bad one winter, the preacher got stuck on his way to church; it on a Sunday and he was going *downhill*. As he sat there spinning his wheels and throwing mud into the air, Walter yelled at him, "Give 'er Hell, Preach."

The Fred House

The Fred House stood near Walter's Curve: with two rooms, a tin roof, vertical plank siding and was "cold as Hell in winter," according to my dad. Fred and Laura had once lived there, but had moved to the other end of the "Big Curve." My brother Warren was born there, December 24, 1934, and Mama called him her "Christmas youngun'."

She planted some cucumber seeds while we lived there, and when they came up, I pulled them out of the ground and asked her to peel them. Even at that young age, I was already showing signs of something, and I never got over the urge to dig in the ground and grow a garden.

Fred's log corncrib was on the Jim's Knob hillside: made of small poles, covered with white oak shingles, and standing on four posts about three feet high. Just up the hill was his orchard and I was told "When them apples fall offa' them trees, boy, just be down yonder at the bottom with a fertilize' sack and catch 'em when they come bouncin' down the hill."

The Fred House spring branch ran under Lambsburg Road near Walter's Curve, and was a handy place to fill boiling car radiators, horses and mules, and on the very hottest days, people sometimes filled themselves. It didn't matter that the spring branch ran through Walter's pasture upstream and it didn't matter that his cows didn't always get out of the branch to do their business.

Everybody knew water got purified when it ran over rocks and sand, and was then safe to drink, no matter where it came from. That had to be true, because somebody read it in the newspaper, and somebody else read it in the bible. Newspapers never lied and anybody who didn't believe in both was off in the head and way above his raising.

The spring branch continued downstream between two high banks, where we played a great game called "Jump The Gulley." While jumping the gulley one day, Benton Marshall's foot slipped on takeoff, and he landed on the other side with his belly hitting the edge of the branch bank. It was funny for everybody but Benton, who wheezed a while, but was soon o k.

Walter's tobacco barn was a great hang out when tobacco was being cured. We roasted apples in the barn flues, dug caves in the road bank, and I got so dirty I was afraid to go home. Dirt and grime just naturally followed me everywhere, every day, and according to Mama, I was the dirtiest youngun' on Stewart's Creek.

Walter and his brother Little Sid were priming tobacco beside the barn, when they got into an argument. One of the two got mad and began priming all the leaves off each stalk. The other one got mad too, and did the same thing. After they completely stripped four rows halfway across the field, it became funny, and they started priming only the ripe leaves again.

Walter Marshall's tobacco barn (2008)

Walter Marshall at age 22 in West Virginia (Courtesy of Nadine Marshall French)

Walter was a big man with a gold tooth that shined brightly when he smiled, and he never hurried. He was a soldier in France in the First World War, and worked in the coalfields in Jenkins Jones, West Virginia in the 1920s.

He called out the West Virginia train stops he'd learned: "Keystone, Kimball, North Fork, Boisevein, Big Vein, Pocahontas and all points north, get aboard please." I could almost see the long coal trains running down the track: with black smoke boiling into the air; "with so many cars it took all day for all of them to go by."

Walter was a farmer who peddled apples, peaches, and garden produce in his 1937 Chevrolet pickup. He said, "My kids won't eat nothin' that don't grow in a paper poke." We sharecropped his cornfields and every other field Pa could find. We were headed for a life of sharecropping, until we bought Jim Smith's farm; we then had more land than we could handle.

The Walter Marshall family (About 1938.)
From the left: Nadine, Verlon, Gaynelle, Lola, Elwood, Walter, Russell, Claude, and Avon.
(Courtesy of Nadine Marshall French, the only surviving member of the above family)

Walter was Fred and Laura Marshall's son, and Lola was Sid Jarrell's daughter, (by his first wife.) Their three youngest kids and my brother Warren and I fought, played, and ran wild in the woods. Verlon was the only one of the seven children who remained in our area when they grew up.

Walter and Lola built their original house in the 1920s. It faced west at the beginning of the Big Curve: with the yard boxed in by boxwoods and pecan trees. When the grass grew high, they "stobbed" the cow to graze, instead of using their reel push mower.

29

The original Walter Marshall home in the early 1940s: with Nadine, Lola, Russell and Gaynell.
(Courtesy of Judy Marshall Fulda and Nadine Marshall French.)

The Marshall home was the end of the line for the school bus and I warmed by their fireplace on cold winter days. My first day of school was in September of 1937, when Mama helped me up into the bus and told the driver, "Take care of my little boy."

Their gasoline-powered washing machine sat on the back porch and made a "putt putt" sound we could hear from our house a mile away: telling us it was washday. Just stomping on a pedal got the contraption cranked, then it washed clothes all by itself. What I liked best was the fact that it burned no wood.

When the Marshall family shot firecrackers at Christmas, Pa answered with his shotgun. He shot into the air and yelled, "Hurrah for Doc. Hatfield, By-Doty. (He had some strange doings and I never knew what he might do next.)

Their son Claude had just got home from the Big War, and was plowing tobacco one hot summer day. He took a break in the shade and told us kids war stories, while the tired mule stood in the field with its head hung down. He stopped in mid sentence and yelled at the mule, "Whoa, Boy," and everybody laughed but the mule.

He chopped the top off his 1939 Ford sedan with an axe and mattock and gave us kids a ride to a nighttime basketball game at Beulah School in his "New Convertible." On the way back, he and Billy Gray Hawks raced side by side for two miles on the two-lane

30

Highway 89. From down in the floor board, I couldn't tell who won, but it was a good thing no cars were going the other way.

Claude said he was riding with an elderly lady to Dan Valley Farms, when she lost control of her car in a curve. When she got it back in the road, she told him, "Don't worry, the Lord is with us." Claude told her, "If He ever was, He jumped out back yonder at that curve."

The Surry County Agricultural Fair came to Mt. Airy in September, and after a long hot summer in the burning fields; most country people were ready for some fun and games. On a "Free-for-school-kids" day, Walter gathered a pickup load of us kids, and we headed for the fair.

There was excitement was in the air, along with the smell of hot dogs, hamburgers, fried onions, and cotton candy. (From long experience, I was an expert at finding food, anywhere.)

There were wonders to behold: Hootchie Kootchie Shows, daredevils who ate fire and nails, juggled bowling pins, swallowed swords, guessed your weight, your grandma's age and promised scary things back-stage. I'd never heard of two-headed calves, wolf men from the jungle, giant lizards and twin-tailed alligators. The only problem: it took some of what I had the least of to go backstage: money.

There were exhibits of farm animals, pies, cakes, crafts, big pumpkins, watermelons and everybody tried to win a ribbon, because it gave them bragging rights until the end of time.

It was said the fair came to town just when people had money from selling tobacco and "some people gambled, help us Lord." Nearly all lost money, but nobody admitted to such nonsense. As they would still be doing decades later, they either broke even or came out ahead. (Since it required money, gambling was never a big problem for my family.)

A new car was given away on Saturday night and everybody with a ticket already had it won. As always, only one person won and when it was given away, the fair ended until next year. I rode back home in the back of Walter's pickup: tired, broke, and sleepy.

The original Marshall home was destroyed by fire in 1944, and was replaced with a one-story. (Gaynell later moved back from Illinois, re-modeled the house, planted an orchard, and raised cattle.) Walter died in 1973, Lola died in 1991, and Gaynell died in 2002.)

31

The Walter Marshall home (2010)

Lambsburg Road continued uphill into the Big Curve, past two sawmill roads on the right. One led across the valley to the Second Knob, where Hurley Smith and I hunted squirrels. When we shot one out of a tree, we had to go to the bottom of the knob to find it. Tarzan often swung on some grapevines in the steep hillsides, and hung on for dear life, because the landing place was also at the bottom of the knob.

The other sawmill road led uphill to a saddleback ridge between Jim's Knob and the Second Knob. We broke ivy and gathered galax leaves in both, and sold them to the T N Woodruff Company at Low Gap. We also gathered the pine knots we used to start fires: the remains of pine trees killed by a wild fire in the 1930s. Mama said after the fire, huckleberries grew everywhere in the knobs.

When Pa and his pals were walking around the Big Curve one day, when they spotted a gallon jug hidden in the leaves. One of the gang "spit out his chew of tobacco and ran to get the jug, which was only a broken one placed there as a joke.

Just beyond the sawmill roads, another road led right to the Bob Faulkner place. Bob built a new log cabin there in 1910, and his daughter, Zula Faulkner Hawks, wrote a book, "Memory Springs" that described living there. She saw her first car there, as it drove by on the Dobson (Lambsburg) Road. They later lived in the John Bates cabin on Bates Hill.

Pa and Mama were picking cherries at the Faulkner place, when a thunderstorm came over the mountain. They took shelter in the old Faulkner cabin, but there were so many fleas inside, they came back out and stayed in the barn until the storm passed.

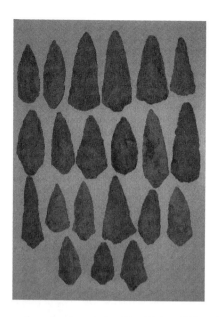

Arrowheads from the Faulkner Woods

While checking out the Faulkner Woods in the 1940s, I found 21 arrowheads piled up beside an old stump. The largest was three inches in length and almost all were larger than those I'd found in the creek bottoms. I searched the whole area, but did not find anymore.

Fisher's Peak from the Bob Faulkner place (2008)

In October of 1975, Helen and I drove to the Faulkner place and made a home movie of hang gliders as they launched from Bald Rock on Fisher's Peak. They sailed around high in the air for a very long time, and finally landed in a pasture near Everette Holder's home in Round Peak. The City of Galax owned the top of the mountain, and eventually stopped the hang gliding due to liability issues.

The Faulkner Road continued along a ridge by H V "Harl" Holder's tobacco barn, his log rental house, and two fishponds, then joined Holder Road near Ivy Green Church.

Lambsburg Road at the Big Curve. (1971)

Back on Lambsburg Road, Fred and Laura Marshall lived in the "Laura House" at the other end of the Big Curve. It was almost exactly like their "Fred House" back at Jim's s Knob: with two rooms, unpainted vertical plank siding and a tin roof. I dimly remember them living there, and us kids sorted through their trash pile.

Walter's son Verlon and his wife Virginia Galyean Thomas Marshall later lived there, and at an even later time, Lawrence Flippen built a brick house on the same spot.

Just beyond the Laura House, a shortcut path by-passed the Big Curve and led back at Walter Marshall's house at the other end. It crossed a swampy area, where we waded and chased tadpoles in the puddles. When the school bus no longer ran to Walter's home, we traveled the path to Mailbox Hill.

A reading class at the Laura House: taught by Sid Jarrell around 1940. L to R: Fred and Laura Marshall, Sid Jarrell, Lola, (sitting) Belle, Walter, Little Sid, and Oscar Marshall. (Courtesy of Nadine Marshall French)

Blue Ridge Baptist Church (2011)

Lambsburg Road continued to the top of the hill, where John Puckett built a dance hall in later years. It was the talk of the county, and ran wide open on weekends, until some free-for-alls with baseball bats and tire chains closed it down. It then became Blue Ridge Baptist Church, and Pa, Mama and a few other locals lost their favorite hangout. (Everybody else agreed it was a change for the better.)

The mail and school bus routes once ended at the bottom of a little knoll we called Mailbox Hill. Several mailboxes there located there until the mail and school bus routes were extended to the state line. A shed made of sawmill slabs kept us out of the wind and rain when we bothered to think about it, but with games to play and races to run, who worried about minor things?

From the top of Mailbox Hill (2008)

Holder Road (later named Tony Holder Road) branched off Lambsburg Road at the foot of Mailbox Hill and led to Harl Holder's huge farm. He owned three rental houses, several tobacco barns and two fishponds, where people paid to fish and attend coon-on-a-log contests.

During a contest, a coon was placed on a log in the middle of the pond, and a dog swam out to fight it. The air was full of shouts, barking and betting and everybody had a great time, including me, until a dog drowned, then I lost much of my enthusiasm.

A gang of adventurous souls sneaked in to the ponds one summer night to ride the rowboats. They were padlocked, but one of our gang could unlock anything with his set of keys. We paddled around in the dark, listened to bullfrogs croak, and had a great time, until someone rocked the boat I was in. It scared the daylights out of me, and being no swimmer, never again did I go boating on Harl's ponds.

In the late 1940s, John and Faith Hawks lived in one of Harl's rental houses, and we rode with them to see the new fire tower on Fisher's Peak. On the way, the universal joint broke in John's 1936 Chevrolet and we walked on to the tower. I made some of my first photographs that day and John walked back to Lambsburg and hired someone to haul us back home. When fire towers fell out of favor in later years, the tower was dismantled and replaced by an F M radio tower. (WBRF Galax, Virginia.)

Fisher's Peak from Holder Road, with the Third Knob at left center and the John Hawks rental house at right center

The Harl and Beatrice Hodge Holder home (2011)

H. V. "Harl" Holder, his wife Beatrice and their kids Nelda, Tyrone, and Tony lived in a big house on Holder Road, with more cattle, hogs, corn, and tobacco than I'd ever seen. While on a visit there, I learned that baby pigs didn't really come from a hollow log, as I'd been told. (The hollow log theory had never made much sense, but I liked it better than the real thing.)

Pa and Harl made moonshine, and in later years, Pa kept his several miles of barbed wire fences repaired. Harl and Beatrice later owned Pine Ridge Lumber Company; built a new house on Highway 89 near Pine Ridge and moved there.

Beatrice Hodge Holder and husband Harl in later years
(Courtesy of Clarence and Nelda Holder Goings)

Holder Road continued by another of Harl's rental houses, climbed what we called Ivy Green Hill (John Moore Hill.) and continued to the Old Low Gap Road: a quarter mile west of Ivy Green Church.

Round Peak Mountain from Mailbox Hill (2008)

I once cleared out a short-cut path (my Tom Hawks Trail) from our house to the bottom of Mailbox Hill and planned to continue the top of Round Peak Mountain, but after chopping down half of the Tom Hawks Woods; the mountain looked fifty miles away. I was already in big-time trouble for using Pa's "good" axe, so my trail ended at Mailbox Hill. At least it by-passed the Big Curve and saved me a lot of foot mileage.

There were no houses on the left side of Lambsburg Road: from the Laura House to Crooked Oak Crossroads. In later years, Frank Coalson's oldest son Bill built a white frame home on top of the hill beyond Mailbox Hill.

The George Easter Road (Watershed Road today)

Just over the hilltop, the George Easter Road led to my grandfather's house down in the valley. Our mailbox was located at the intersection, until the mail route was extended to the state line. We seldom got mail and didn't check by very often. When Surry County named every road, cow path and driveway, the George Easter Road became Watershed Road and I was very disappointed.

Linc Gardner's "New House" (2011)

Just beyond the George Easter Road, another road (later named Sawmill Lane) led left to the house Linc Gardner built when his first one burned. He died in 1935, and with nobody living there for many years, the area grew up in weeds, grass, broom straw, and blackberry briers. It was sad to see such a nice home and feed barn going to waste. His huge Gardner Woods were another story. I grew up a mile away and almost lived there: hunting, prowling, and searching for gold.

The Gardner Road continued to the homes of Benton Seal, Josie Seal, and Clarence and Lizzie Seal Hawks near what we called the "Old Seal House" on Stewart's Creek.

Frank and Mary Coalson lived beyond the Gardner Road, in what began as a one-room log cabin. As the family increased, more rooms were added, the outside walls were covered with planks and weatherboard, and the roof was covered with tin.

Their well was close the road and every traveler that came by, drank the cold water and rested in the shade. Like every other well in the country, it had "the coldest water in the country."

Frank and family were farmers and woodcutters, and owned many acres of woods. A huge pile of stove wood was always waiting to be hauled to Mount Airy on Frank's Dodge pickup. When Grandpa quit driving his horse and wagon to town; he often rode with Frank on Saturdays to sell butter and eggs on Market Street.

They owned 65 acres of land in The Knobs, and in 1962, Helen and I bought ten acres from them on top of Jim's Knob, and in 1968, we bought the remaining 55 acres. (We made land payments to Frank and Mary for many years.)

Jim's Knob was one of my favorite places when growing up and we planned to build a house there and move back to the country. We built a road, drilled a well, got electricity, installed a septic tank, and bought a house trailer for a weekend getaway. We bought house plans, set fruit trees and were moving right along, until a winter came along with so much snow, we couldn't drive up the knob for weeks.

I learned right away that climbing the knob in a foot of snow on foot was nowhere near as funny as it was when growing up. That one winter brought an end to our big plans, but our son Mike and his wife Pam later built a new house on top of the knob.

Frank and Mary were friendly hard working people who lived close to the land. Frank was a soldier in World War One and except for talking about the cold and mud; he didn't talk much about war.

Frank and Mary Coalson's home

Their children were: Bill, Pauline, Brady, Edith, Hoover, Charlie, Harold, twin girls Mary and Sarah, and the youngest, Carroll. (Buster.) Harold was a passenger when I wrecked my second car, and we were drafted into the army on the same day: April 28, 1953.

The Coalsons farmed with mules, which were said to be as stubborn as mules. You had to build a fire under one to get it started and if that didn't work, a good, solid whack between the eyes with a 2 x 4 just might do the trick.

If mules were any harder to work with than horses were with Pa, my family would've starved. When plowing, the horse sometimes ran sideways and demolished a row of corn or tobacco. He and the horse then had a meeting of the minds and even more crops got destroyed. I think Pa wiped out more stuff than the horse but he always won the war.

Frank sometimes rode his mule to our house and he and Pa checked out the weather forecasts inside the granary. It worked best there, because Pa had a jug hidden behind the meat box. Most of the important work was done inside, but they came outside often to check the sky, the wind direction and other factors. It was a serious business that had to be done just right.

I played Roy Acuff's "Great Speckled Bird" record over and over on their floor model wind-up phonograph, until I memorized it. I was already a great singer, and could hardly wait to get on the Grand Old Opry and make my fortune.

We borrowed a table model wind-up phonograph from my aunt and my brother and I played the worn-out scratchy records continually. It came with a handful of steel needles that never wore out, but we changed them often. (How could anybody know how good we were at technical things, unless they saw us in action?) We played the records until we finished driving our parents mad.

Frank and Mary Coalson picking blackberries

(In later years, the Mt Airy News ran a story about Frank and Mary still working their garden, along with a photo of Frank still plowing with his mule.) He died in1980 and Mary died in 1986.

My brother Warren fixed up an old jalopy, and became the terror of the backwoods. It had no muffler and you could hear it coming a mile away. He wore out the George Easter Road and sometimes sneaked out on Lambsburg Road.

The highlight of his day was seeing how far into the woods he could throw gravel in Frank Coalson's Curve. (He said he moved more gravel than the Highway Department.) With very few cars on the roads, he never ran into anybody and never got caught.

Gid and Ila Willey lived beyond Frank's curve in a tin-roofed house on the right: with a fenced-in garden beside the road and a well in the back yard. Their cherry trees hung over the road and cherries sometimes disappeared when a certain person walked by.

The Gid and Ila Willey home

Ila and Gid Willey

Few people in our world could afford a car or pickup, let alone a garage, but Gid parked his International pickup in a log garage. He was one of the neighbors who helped build barns and houses, and as was said about he and Ila, "They're hard workers, and they don't bother nobody."

Gid, Pa, and other men sometimes "graveled" for fish by feeling under rocks and roots in Stewart's Creek. When Gid stuck his hand under a rock one day, a mud turtle almost bit his finger off. I was a brave soul, but no way would I stick my hand under a rock in the creek.

The Willey's son Charlie once brought a young rabbit to school in a cardboard box. I wondered how he caught it, because I could never run fast enough to catch one. Gid died in 1972, when he fell off a house he was working on, and Ila died in 1989.

Around another curve beyond Gid's house, another Gardner Road also led to the Linc Gardner house. One memorable summer, Pa let me grow my own small patch of tobacco, and I made enough money to buy my first and only bicycle.

I was "all grown-up," and insisted on riding it the twelve miles back home from Mt Airy, and was doing a great job until I got near the Gardner Road. When a car came speeding around the curve, I got excited and wrecked. The driver stopped to see if I was hurt, but the only thing hurt was my pride.

Wagon train on the Lambsburg (Pine Ridge) road in 1971

A log tobacco barn stood close to the Gardner Road, and a woman was killed there in 1889 when her horse ran away and her wagon hit a tree. According to my brother Curtis, she (Elizabeth H. Snow) was probably the first person buried in Zion Hill Cemetery at Crooked Oak Church.

Lambsburg Road continued around the curve to Crooked Oak Crossroads, where it became Pine Ridge Road. Old Low Gap Road on the left was later named Maple Grove Church Road and the road on the right remained Old Low Gap Road. (Because of where it led, we called it "Round Peak Road.")

Crooked Oak Crossroads (2008)

Beginning at Oscar Marshall's Old House back on Stewart's Creek and ending at Crooked Oak Crossroads lived the people we were most involved with in our everyday lives: our friends, neighbors and kin people, with whom we swapped sugar, flour, coffee, tools, news, and stuff we grew on the farm.

In the early years, we lived rent-free in the rental houses of Walter and Oscar Marshall and sharecropped their fields. We broke ivy, pulled galax leaves and cut fishing poles in their woods, and when we found a bee tree on their land, we shared their own honey with them. As my dad said it, "They's Marshalls ever' which a' way you look in these woods."

The Crossroads

Chapter 3

Road to Pine Ridge

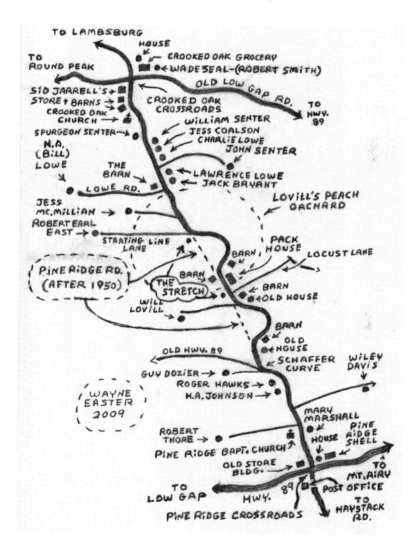

Road to Pine Ridge

At one time, there were small country stores at almost every country crossroads: where locals gathered to "shoot the breeze," and solve world problems. Since flour, coffee and sugar didn't grow very well on red-dirt farms, people "went down to the store," and traded stuff they grew for stuff they couldn't grow.

They sat around the wood heater in winter, swapped lies and gossip, drank "sody pop, ate Moon Pies and Nabs and smoked "roll-your-own Golden Grain cigarettes. In summer, they sat outside and grew some of the best crops ever, and never got out of the shade.

A drawing of Sid Jarrell's Store

Sid Jarrell's small country store was one of those. It stood in the southwest corner of Crooked Oak Crossroads: an unpainted, tin roofed frame building that was only open part-time. When someone stopped by, Sid called from his house next door, "Be there in a minute."

Sid was getting on in years and was never in a hurry, which was no big problem, because most people in our world had more time than money, nowhere to go and all day to get there. Kelly Senter, who could talk just like Sid, hid behind the store one day and when someone stopped out front, Kelley yelled, "Be there in a minute."

Sid was a schoolteacher who never owned a car, but walked all over our country: teaching older people to read. He came by our house in the late 1930s, carrying an armload of books: on his way to a neighbor's home to give a reading lesson. Everybody who knew him said, "Sid's a good old man." He died in 1956.

Sid's two log tobacco barns stood on the right side of Pine Ridge Road: a few hundred feet beyond the crossroads. The second barn was so close to the road, it was dangerous to be out front when a car came by. It was a favorite loafing place, and at tobacco curing time, a crowd gathered in to make music and tell tall tales, while us kids listened bug-eyed.

One memorable Sunday, the usual crowd was there, telling tall tales, when John Hull came driving up Pine Ridge Road in a cloud of dust. He slid to a stop in his Flat-headed Ford V8 coupe, leaned out the window and the tall tales continued, while everybody drooled on his car: wishing they had one just like it.

The dust had just settled when Ed Smith drove up in his International pick-up and stopped beside John's car. Ed was a magistrate, and was trying to arrest John for speeding, drinking or doing something illegal. He said, "Stop that thing, John!"

John, who was still sitting in his car, didn't "stop that thing," but sped off and threw gravel all over everybody. He turned right at Crooked Oak Crossroads in another cloud of dust and went out of sight down Old Low Gap Road. I hadn't yet learned the consequences of breaking the law, but I knew I wanted a Ford just like it.

John said he drank a whole quart of moonshine one day, and ate a whole pound of hot dogs "right out of the pack." As he told it, "Them damn hot dogs might near killed me."

He drove the same Ford pickup for many years and my son Mike asked him if it was ever going to wear out. John told Mike he was going to take it with him when he "went. (He later had a heart attack and died while driving the pickup. It stopped with the accelerator pressed all the way to the floorboard, and the engine ran full-throttle until it failed.)

Crooked Oak Primitive Baptist Church (established July 1878) was just beyond Sid Jarrell's tobacco barns on the right side of Pine Ridge Road. The official name was Zion Hill but most people called it Crooked Oak. The white frame building had three windows on each side, a tin roof, and two out houses out back. It was blazing hot inside in summer, and ice cold in winter: even with a wood heater going full-blast.

Foot Washing Day came on the fourth Sunday in July. It was the high social event of summer, and the one day of the year when everybody went to church: including Pa, Mama and us boys.

Crooked Oak/Zion Hill Church

People came from all over to the annual gathering at the little white church on Pine Ridge Road. From Scrap-town, Garbrawley, Flower Gap, Lambsburg, Pine Ridge, Round Peak, Beulah and Low Gap they came, along the hot dusty roads: riding in "A" models, "T" models and a few newer models. By farm wagon, buggy, horseback, muleback, bicycle and on foot they came, and all wore their Sunday best.

The meeting came at just the right time of the year: giving everybody a welcome break from the never-ending grind of tending corn and tobacco fields in the hottest part of summer. Most people hadn't seen each other since the last Foot Washing or the last funeral and had a huge backlog of gossip, jokes, and news waiting to be swapped.

The kids and dogs chased each other in the dust and dirt until their clothes were all the same color. The women wore homemade, slatted cardboard sunbonnets; ankle length dresses, and fanned them-selves with cardboard fans from Moody's Funeral Home. They talked about their families, their gardens, how many green beans they'd "put up," and gossiped about the women not there.

The men wore new bib overalls, and carried wind-up pocket watches in the bib pockets; with the chains hanging out. They' chawed 'baccer, dipped snuff, and smoked "roll your own" Golden Grain cigarettes. Anyone who "ran out" of "store-boughten" tobacco, "rolled his own" from his own tobacco, and told nobody.

The air was a cloud of tobacco smoke and the ground was a sea of tobacco juice, as they traded guns, knives, horses, cows, mules, and told tall tales of the good old days. The more they talked about the old days, the better they became and no way would anybody ever stretch the truth. (It was hard to imagine wading six feet of snow when you were only four feet tall and going uphill both ways.)

Some their best farming of the year was done on Foot-washing Sunday, "right there under the oak trees." A never-ending discussion was held about whose horse could out-pull whose mule and whose could run the fastest. "My mule can smell rain coming and your horse can't."

Everybody there had the best damn coon or foxhound ever put on God's Green Earth: "My ol' Blue treed a coon one time and clomb' right up that tree after it. That ol' coon come a' fallin' out scared to death and seein' ol' Blue up that tree about scared me to death too. He run a fox one time for two days, all around Skull Camp Mountain and Round Peak and Fishers Peak and the Sugar Loaf, and if I hadn't a' shot 'im, he'd a' still been runnin'."

One memorable Foot Washing Day in the 1940s, a redheaded girl from Lambsburg stole the whole show. She came dressed as a cowgirl: complete with cowboy hat and two six-guns on her gun-belt. She was an instant hit with all the men and if prizes had been given, she would've won everything in sight. Even without a horse, she was the center of attention and I was impressed too, because I'd never seen a real live cowgirl. The women were not impressed.

Zion Hill Cemetery

Zion Hill Cemetery was just across the road, and on Foot Washing Sunday, Frank Coalson parked his Dodge pickup there in the shade of an oak tree. He sold ice cream cones and cups of lemonade from a

51

brand new galvanized washtub that had a big block of ice floating in it. Pa said Frank's lemonade was, "Made in the shade, stirred with a spade, best ol' lemonade that's ever been made." I agreed and could've put away the whole tub-full all by myself, *and* the ice cream.

Frank Coalson's lemonade tree (2008)

A few men sampled fruit jars hidden in the woods, and as the day went on, they became experts on everything under the sun. Their gardens, corn and tobacco crops got bigger and better and some almost became millionaires right there in broad daylight. Those who drank too much "rested" a while and snored a while, while their wives threatened to "burn them woods to the ground and everybody in there."

The preaching, foot washing, and singing took up way too much time, and the song Amazing Grace lasted for at least an hour. When my Grandma Easter sang, she sang highest and loudest, then all the dogs howled, then all the kids howled, then everybody laughed.

Except for some lemonade and ice cream, I'd had nothing to eat for at least a week and was about on my last legs. "Don't they know people starve to death if they don't eat? All that preachin', prayin', singin' and foot washin's a' waste a' time and they might forget all about eatin' and all them cakes and pies might go bad. They should'a washed their feet last night like I had to do after wadin' them mud holes. At least the graveyard's right across the road if anybody dies of starvation."

After what seemed like a week, the meeting came to an end: just before I did. Every family had brought baskets and dishes of food from home and the long wooden tables were filled with more good stuff to eat than I'd ever seen.

There were cakes and pies as far as the eye could see and every chicken in the country must have been fried and brought there. (If other people's chickens were as hard to catch as ours, there were some mighty tired people at the meeting. Our chickens ran free, and when we wanted one to eat, we had to run it down, which usually took the whole family and the dog.)

For all the kids and some grownups, it was the biggest and best meal of the year. Nobody cared how much anybody ate and since next year was a long time down the road, I took no chances. No way would I go home hungry.

It had been slow day, until the eating began, then it was "Katy Bar the Door," and the sun raced across the sky toward Fisher's Peak. In almost no time, all the food was gone, all the big tales had been told and everybody headed back down the long dusty roads to home. It was a sad time, because Foot-washing Days at Crooked Oak Church were special and should last forever.

Just beyond the church, Ed Smith's cow pasture cornered on Pine Ridge Road: where he fed his cows and a bull. Like every other bull I ever heard of, his was a mean one. When it shook its head, I headed for high ground, and when it pawed the ground and bawled, I poured on more coal and headed for even higher ground.

Rumor had it that people brought their cows to Ed's pasture for a visit at certain times of the year. Nobody told me why; because that was stuff us kids didn't need to know about. Somehow, long before old age set in, I finally figured it out. That was where Pa and Grandpa took their cows when they left home leading them with a rope. (At the time, I thought they might just be going for a stroll along the road.)

Pine Ridge Road continued beyond Ed's pasture and tobacco field to an area known as "Easy Street." As legend and a few angry housewives told it, people who lived there were lazy and didn't work. All they did was loaf, play music, drink likker' and dance all night "down yonder at that old barn." (If that meant they didn't have to hoe corn and tobacco in the hot summer fields, they were my kind of people.) As I found out later, most were hard workers, just like everybody else.)

Spurgeon and Minnie Senter lived in a white frame house on the right: the first house on Easy Street: It was the only close-to-the-road house on the right, all the way from Crooked Oak Crossroads to the Schaffer Curve near Pine Ridge. Their kids were Arlene, Aldine, Doris, and Louis. Spurgeon was one of the Easy Street Musicians, where everybody played something: a banjo, fiddle, "juice harp," harmonica or all four.

William and Nan Senter lived beyond Spurgeon's in a log house under some white pines: with a yard surrounded by boxwoods, grape vines and bee gums. He was getting on in years and no longer farmed, but sold honey and the best moonshine on Easy Street. He kept it hidden behind a log in the woods across Pine Ridge Road, and when the right person came along, William crossed the road and found exactly what the customer wanted.

A better hiding place would've been under his bee gums, because bees and bee gums certainly kept me out of Grandpa's best grapes. Pa said, "The law's "gonna' walk on William's log one day," but it never happened

William had a cable and pulley system that brought water from his spring far down in the valley. A bucket mounted on pulleys rolled downhill along the cable to the spring, and when it filled up with water, he wound it back up-hill to the house. It was a fine piece of machinery and beat the heck out of totin' water up a steep hill.

On a Saturday night to remember, William's barn ran out into the road in front of a passing car. It was a true story, because the car owner swore to God he was in the middle of the road when he wrecked. Another night (on Halloween) William's wagon dismantled itself and got back together on top of the barn and nobody had any idea how. (I kept a close eye on William's barn.)

Jess and Eleanor Coalson lived beyond William: on the same side of the road. Their four children were girls: Shelby, Margaret, Phyliss and Pat. Unlike most of our neighbors, Jess didn't farm, but worked in Mt. Airy five days a week.

Jess learned about power car windows one day at Crooked Oak Crossroads. When he pushed a button in someone's new car, a back window rolled down. He whirled around to see what was happening, then pushed another button and did the same thing when a different window opened. (It was out-of-this-world funny for us kids, who were so much smarter than grown-ups.)

Charlie and his wife "Doaney" Lowe lived next door in a white frame house, where two rows of boxwoods bordered their cement walk: the only one on Easy Street. Their daughter Fannie married Elmer Hawks, who went away to the Big War and never came back.

Charlie was one of the early Easy Street musicians, and his home was headquarters for jam sessions. He, Tommy Jarrell, Fred Cockerham, and others often played at all-night dances all around the country.

I remember attending two of the dances with my parents: one at Bill Puckett's home on Old Low Gap Road and another at Coy Cockerham's home on Walker Hollow Road in Round Peak. (We stayed all night at the Bill Puckett dance.)

The Charlie and Donna Lowe home (1987)

A dance was held at someone's home almost every weekend, except for a two-week period beginning in mid-December. They were then held every night until the New Year, and they called it "Breakin' up Christmas."

There was almost no trouble until more automobiles brought in outsiders who brought fights, shootings, and other problems, which almost brought an end to the all-night dances.

55

Charley, Fred, and Tommy's unique style of playing became known as Round Peak Music. Several bands: including the Camp Creek Boys, Earnest East and the Pine Ridge Boys, and Benton Flippen and the Smoky Valley Boys contributed to the reputation of Round Peak Music and the style eventually became known nationwide.

As Grady Hawks did on Bates Hill some 20 years earlier, an older Charlie Lowe sat on his front porch in the 1940s and picked his claw hammer banjo for the whole world to hear. He died in 1964.

Fred Cockerham played on radio stations with different bands and worked in Norfolk Virginia during the Big War. He returned home to Low Gap and a cataract operation on both eyes in 1960 left him almost completely blind. He continued playing the fiddle and another operation in 1970 brought back much of his sight. He died in 1980.

Tommy Jarrell quit playing for many years, but after retiring from driving a motor grader for the state, he began playing again. People then came from far away places to his home on South Franklin Road in Mount Airy to learn his way of playing the fiddle. Tommy died in 1985.

The John Senter home

Just past Charlie's house, a driveway led to John Senter's log house down on the hillside. John's dad Phillip originally built the house, which was much larger than ordinary log houses.

Two of John's two daughters, Ellen and Lucinda, were my schoolmates and we rode the same bus to Beulah School. John was an inventive soul who became the idol of neighborhood kids when he drove his goat-powered cart to the store at Crooked Oak Crossroads.

His two sons, Willie and Kelly were in the Big War and John said Willie was "makin' a killin' tradin' knives in the army." Both made it back home safely in the mid-1940s and were two of the great clowns on Easy Street. Kelly told about someone's cat that drowned in a crock of molasses. He said, "You know, they wasted nearly all them 'lasses gittin' that dead cat out."

Back on Pine Ridge Road, Charlie Lowe's son Lawrence (another musician) and his wife Dorothy lived beyond the John Senter driveway. Most men I knew were farmers or saw-millers but like Jess Coalson, Lawrence "worked in town" and made music. Their kids were Woltz, Jack and Jackie.

Jack and Annie Bryant lived beyond the Lawrence Lowe house. He was a farmer who owned a dump truck and hauled dirt and gravel. He was also a foxhunter who parked his Dodge pickup at the state line on Saturday nights, and listened to his foxhounds run in the Knobs. Their kids were Ina Mae, Lester Ray and Debra. Ina Mae and I graduated from Beulah School in 1950, and Lester Ray drove my school bus during my last year of school. (I passed the school bus driver's test, but never drove one on a route.)

Just across Pine Ridge Road was a legend known far and wide: a dilapidated log tobacco barn called "The Barn." It leaned southwest, leaked and had seen better days, but it still did its job and did it well.

As the grapevine had it, "All them people that hang around down yonder at that old barn is shiftless and lazy and all they do is mess around, make music, drink moonshine and play poker and make a big racket all night long."

For some, including my dad, (according to Mama) it was their doghouse, their second home: their home away from home. It generated fire and brimstone sermons in local churches and a group of housewives threatened to "burn the whole mess to the ground."

After a hard week in the mines and cornfields, it was time to play, and play they did. From Round Peak, Pine Ridge, Lambsburg, Low Gap, and all over they came on weekends: to the worn-out log barn on Easy Street, at the intersection of Lowe and Pine Ridge Roads.

They played poker, the claw-hammer banjo, fiddle and harmonica. They drank R C Colas, ate Moon Pies and shared some of "Round Peak's best from right up yonder under Fisher's Peak."

They talked about the good old days, who had been caught doing what, and whom they did it with. They told of strange doings, like the time William Senter's barn ran out into the street in front of a car. The old men talked about the good old days when they owned the world, and younger men talked about women and tomorrow when the world would be theirs.

On occasion, the law stopped by and a miracle happened right there in broad daylight. The cards, money and moonshine vanished into thin air and the Barn became a house of worship. When asked what they were doing there, the answer was, "We're holding a little prayer service here, Sheriff; don't you see that sign up there on the wall that says, "Easy Street Church of God? (Before the sheriff drove out of sight, prayer service got under way again, better than ever.

Everybody had a great time, but those who had just got home from the Big War had the best time of all. They'd seen Germany, Paris, Tokyo and the South Sea Islands and all agreed, there was no place like home and Easy Street.

Lightning never struck the barn and nobody burned it down, but old age finally brought it to an end. Mama said Pa and some other long-time members "lost their main home and had nowhere to go, poor souls"

G C Lovill's Peach Orchard began just beyond the barn: on both sides of Pine Ridge Road. When the trees bloomed in spring, it became a sea of pink, but during growing season, they were sprayed with something that smelled "worser' than a dead mule." Nobody hung out near the orchard on Spraying Day.

A driveway on top of the hill led right to the home of Robert Earl East. He was picked on far too much by other school kids, until he whacked a heckler with his book satchel and cured the problem. He grew up, became a tobacco farmer and saw-miller, and the Oscar Marshall family hired him to cut the "biggest pine tree in the country" at their Old Place on Stewart's Creek.

Pine Ridge Road curved left across from the driveway, and circled around through the orchard. It was a bumpy road and a mean ride for the school bus and bicycles, but never got muddy in winter.

The "Stretch" in 2008

The road was paved in 1950, the curves were eliminated, and the new part was named "The Stretch." Young men and a few older men who never grew up, met there on Saturday nights to test their driving abilities and hot rods. Lookouts were posted at both ends to keep innocent drivers from harm's way, and watch for the law.

I ran my first and only drag race there in 1955. I'd just got home from the army and was ready to ride. My partner and I ran side by side for a quarter mile, until I lost my nerve and the race at the same time. (He also had the best car.) When Surry County named all the roads, the Robert Earl East driveway became "Starting Line Lane."

In the summer of 1950, I'd been out of high school for a few weeks and still hadn't made my fortune. I'd known all along that my 12 years at Beulah School would eventually pay off and sure enough it happened. I began picking peaches at Lovill's Peach Orchard and the big money was about to come rolling in. With all that money, I'd buy a car, travel, and maybe even hire somebody to do the work, while I lived on Easy Street.

Jess Mc.Millian (the foreman) said the peach pickers could eat all the peaches they wanted. He'd never met anybody like me or he would not have said that. From long experience, I knew good food when I saw it and dinner was hanging all over the peach trees. No doubt about it, I could eat as many as I picked, all day long.

Sure enough, the first half-dozen were out of this world and I said to myself, "Where else can you get rich and eat at the same time? All of my friends should be so lucky."

59

Before very long, peaches didn't taste so good anymore and when I looked around, nobody else was eating peaches either. Maybe there was something I didn't know; maybe that dead-mule spray hurt the taste, or something.

July tobacco fields were said be the hottest places on Earth, but when peach fuzz and sweat began eating me alive, I wondered about that. Even fifty cents an hour no longer sounded so good. I looked all around, but none of my fellow pickers had even raised a sweat, and here I was about to kick the bucket. To avoid looking like the weakling I was, I managed to hang on to what turned out to be a very long day.

Just before quitting time, Jess held up a finger, looked at his pocket watch, and counted down. (Everybody had already quit working: just waiting for him to pull the trigger.) At the top of the hour, he said something that became famous on Easy Street: "That's it, boys." The sun had never looked better as it set behind Fisher's Peak and I headed back home to Mama and supper.

The peach orchard pack house was on the left side of the road going toward Pine Ridge, and it looked cool and inviting. Those who worked there didn't have to bake their brains in the boiling sun like I was doing.

The pack house, (From a home movie in the 1980s)

Someone must've been watching over me, because Jess then put me to work grading peaches in the pack house. Working in the shade was a great change, but when I went to bed at night, I could still see peaches with my eyes closed. After two weeks of torture, I gave up the big money and went back to the tobacco fields: knowing peaches would not be my life's work.

The peach orchard was a Lover's Lane until peach picking time. Then, when a car stopped anywhere in the area, it got checked out by a night watchman. Some of the local boys made his life miserable, as they parked beside the orchard and turned off their car lights. When the watchman cranked up and came their way, they drove off: repeating the process several times. Like me, they probably didn't even like peaches. (As far as I know, the watchman never caught anyone stealing peaches.)

In later years, the peach trees wore out, the orchard came to an end, and the pack house was used to store hay, until a case of arson brought it to an end.

Before I began driving, the sun was just coming up one Sunday morning, as I walked west along Pine Ridge Road by an old tobacco barn that stood just beyond the pack house: about where I77 and Pine Ridge Volunteer Fire department are today.

I'd been to the Owl Show (a late-Saturday-night movie) in Mt. Airy the night before, and when the hour got very late, I couldn't thumb a ride, and began walking home. Not a single car passed me in either direction all the way back.

A twelve-mile hike was, to say the least, a long one, and I was completely worn out when I got back, and it being a Sunday, I slept all day. Even a monkey learns by repetition, and when the same thing happened again, I slept in a parked taxi on the corner of Main and Pine Streets.

Will and Ada Lovill lived in a white house off the road on the right, beyond today's I77. Their sons were Cleve and Ben. Pine Ridge Road originally curved left at the Lovill Road and came back into the area of a present-day "Town and Country" housing development. John Hull lived across from the Lovill Road and Cleve Lovill later built a new brick home nearby.

Just past the Lovill place, Pine Ridge Road dipped into a small hollow, where every vehicle that came by got stuck in knee-deep mud, including the school bus. When we got stuck, we just sat there and pouted until someone pulled us out. On one occasion, the driver dropped the dipstick down into the carburetor air intake, which overrode the engine governor and we got unstuck.

I watched the machinery grade Pine Ridge Road for paving in 1950. The Lovill and peach orchard curves were then eliminated and the road became a super highway for bicycles.

61

An old two-story frame house stood on the left beyond the mud hole. Cuban Thomas was killed in a car wreck there in 1942: a few days before he was scheduled to leave for the army. He was the son of Cleve and Zelphia Thomas, who lived across Stewart's Creek from us.

Schaffer Curve (2009)

While riding my bicycle one Sunday, I met Garnet Golding, who was driving very fast down Pine Ridge Road. He slid off Schaffer Curve onto Old Highway 89 and headed west in a cloud of dust.

A state trooper, who was chasing Garnett, got stuck when he took a shortcut across a plowed field. Garnett was probably hauling a load of moonshine, but he got away, and I decided he could drive almost as well as John Hull. (At that time, all of my heroes drove hot rods and made the dust fly.)

Just after I got home from the army, I was driving home one night and "pouring on the coal," as us experts were known to do. I slid off Highway 89 onto Pine Ridge Road, and made a bunch of tire noise.

A state trooper (Josh Howell) chased me down near Schaffer Curve, and asked me, "Where in Hell's the fire, Son?" He didn't give me a ticket, but gave me a nice long lecture about speeding. I drove on home with a halo hanging over my head as big as a washtub: far below the speed limit. (I'd thought all along Josh was grinning behind his ears.)

Guy Dozier, who lived beside Schaffer Curve, owned Pine Ridge Shell Service Station on Highway 89. (In 1982; his son Exton leased it to our son Mike.) Roger Hawks lived in the next house on the

62

right and just around the next curve lived H A (Sawmill) Johnson and family in the former Pine Ridge School building: one of the two schools Mama attended.

The former Pine Ridge School building

Their son Donald played the best guitar I'd ever heard and I tried to play just like him, but best I could do, my guitar playing sounded like beating on Mama's washtub. During a play at Beulah School, Professor "Fess" Robertson told me to go into his office, turn on the intercom and play a tune for the audience. I knew I couldn't play very well, but figured it might be a step up the ladder on my way to Nashville.

I was doing my very best on one of my very best tunes, when he came running into the office and told me to stop. I later decided my playing was so bad it was funny to the audience. (I'm still waiting for Nashville to call.)

Pine Ridge Baptist Church today

Pine Ridge Baptist Church and cemetery were on the right beyond the Johnson house. (It would later be located across the road on the left.) A driveway led right to Robert Thore's home back off the road: in the area of today's Mountain Lumber Company. Mary Marshall, her son Bud and daughter Irene lived in an ancient store building that stood very close to the road, and a blacksmith shop and the John Gardner store once stood nearby.

Pine Ridge Crossroads

Pine Ridge Road crossed Highway 89 at the intersection and continued to Haystack Road and the county seat of Dobson. Pine Ridge Post Office was once stood on the right beyond the intersection.

Pine Ridge Post Office, built about 1860
(Courtesy of the Surry County Historical Society)

Turning left on Highway 89 led to Pine Ridge Shell Station on the left: a white frame building with a two-story frame house beside it. Reid Flippen and his wife Bernice lived there when they owned the store.

An outback storage building became headquarters on Election Day, and a free ride and moonshine were available for anyone who wanted to vote. My dad had no automobile, but had no trouble getting there. He must've done lots of voting, because he got there early and stayed until someone brought him home far in the night: loaded to the gills.

The store sold groceries and Shell gasoline and became known as Pine Ridge Shell. As time passed, the original wood building was replaced with a much larger one, and had several different owners over the years, including our son Mike.

Even after Shell gasoline was no longer sold at the store, the name remained. Like Crooked Oak Grocery and so many other rural store buildings, it now stands empty: another victim of the times.

The Pine Ridge Store in 1934
Courtesy of Don Holder (shown with his dad)

Pine Ridge Shell in the 1980s

Chapter 4
Old Low Gap Road East

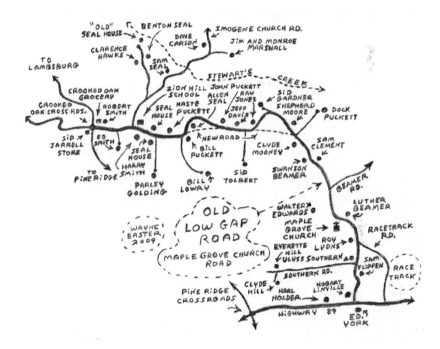

Crooked Oak Crossroads

Old Low Gap Road East

Crooked Oak Grocery

Wade and Pat Seal Pat built Crooked Oak Grocery in 1949: in the opposite corner from Sid Jarrell's Store. It was a larger building, with groceries and gas and became a popular hangout for the whole community.

For some locals, including my dad, a trip "down to the store." was the highlight of the day. They gathered around the woodstove in winter, drank "little-bottle Co' Colers'," smoked cigarettes, "chawed 'baccer," and shot the breeze. In summer, they sat outside in the shade, and anyone who didn't come by got talked about in detail.

Levi Murphy was there most days and kids were unmerciful in playing tricks on him. He was an older, friendly man who took the ribbing with a big smile. My brother Warren told about someone clearing land with a bulldozer near an old well. When Levi asked what they were doing, Warren told him they were getting ready to move the well. In later years, a hospital nurse asked Warren his name; he told her he was Levi Murphy.

Some local drivers spun their vehicles in circles at the intersection to see how far they could throw gravel. After the roads were paved, they spun figure eights and tried to stay on the pavement. Those who did it best, made the best figure eights, left the biggest black marks and bought new tires most often. In the early 1950s, I bought a set of re-caps on credit for my first car. At $5.00 per week, they were worn out before they were paid for.

When Robert and Ethel Smith bought the store in 1961, my dad became part of the furnishings. Any day he made it "down to the store," for his "little-bottle sody' pop and seegar" he'd had a good day. The store closed for good in 1992, and for the first time in memory, there was no longer a loafing place at Crooked Oak Crossroads.

The Ed and Grace Smith home (2008)

A driveway a half-mile east of the crossroads led by a small cemetery to the home of Ed and Grace Easter Smith. (Aunt Grace was my Dad's sister: George and Alice Easter's oldest child.)

They owned a huge farm and dairy and in the early years, we swapped tobacco primings. I drank my first refrigerated milk at their house, and saw right away I was going to like it.

Most people I knew either carried water from a spring or wound it from a well, but the Smith family had a water pump. They just opened a spigot inside the house and water came pouring out. That was even better than carrying water downhill like Sam Coalson back on the creek.

I met electricity head-on by touching an ungrounded outside water spigot behind their house. My arm got numb all the way to my elbow and my mouth tasted like licking rusty iron. How could something you couldn't see sneak up on you and hurt you?

I took my first bike ride in their yard and it was a total disaster. Everything was going great, until I collided with a washtub full of ice water that had a watermelon cooling in it. The tub turned over and everything: bicycle, watermelon, and myself, landed on the ground. The only thing not bent was the watermelon.

The Ed Smith family in the 1950s
(Courtesy of Dorothy Smith Hicks.)

In front, l-r: Ray, Aunt Grace, Ed, and Robert. In back l-r: Gay, Vera, Harry, Dorothy and Ina. Ina and I graduated from Beulah School in 1950.

One day in fall of the year, we helped them make molasses beside the spring. The cane stalks were fed into a mill operated by a mule that walked in circles around it. After the juice was squeezed out, they poured it into a vat and cooked it for hours. As it cooked, a skim formed on top that they kept skimmed off. When the juice finally thickened into molasses, they poured it into canning jars and we went back home with a whole load of 'lasses.

Another great thing at their house was a June apple tree in the meadow: with apples that ripened early in the year and nobody cared how many I ate. (When I77 came through in later years, it ran through the area where the apple tree once stood.)

Ed's International pickup had one unbent fender and he bent that one when he ran into a tobacco sled. One of his kids told him, "Daddy, that was the good fender." According to Ethel Calloway Smith, we rode in the pickup on a chinquapin hunt across the mountain in September 1946. Ed was fatally injured in a farm tractor accident at home in 1972, and Aunt Grace died in 1991.

Zion Hill School

The Zion Hill School building was on the left beyond Ed's driveway: at the intersection of Imogene Church and Old Low Gap Roads. Pa, his brother and sisters and most of our older neighbors attended school in the big frame building.

On occasion, some kids rode a mule or horse to school, but most walked through the woods or along the roads and brought their lunch in a tin lard can. Somebody replaced the sausage ball in a boy's biscuit with what a horse left on the road. (Nobody ever found out who did it, but it may have been Pa.)

Some of our older neighbors never attended school, but Pa attended Zion Hill, and Mama attended Oakland School on Bryant Road and Pine Ridge School at Pine Ridge. When school was no longer taught at Zion Hill, the building became a rental house and when I-77 came through, it crossed Old Low Gap Road exactly where the schoolhouse once stood. The intersection was then moved, as well as the Clarence Hawks Road, and Imogene Church Road eventually became West Imogene Church Road.

A few hundred feet down Imogene Church Road, the Clarence Hawks Road branched left to the homes of Clarence and Lizzie Seal Hawks, her brother Benton Seal's home and what we called the "Old Seal House" on the banks of Stewart's Creek. William Golding built the house in the 1800s, and Lizzie and Josie's parents bought it about 1919 and moved there from the Haystack Road area.

The "Old Seal House"

I grew up just up the creek, and hunted and prowled the huge Gardner Woods that joined the Seal property. Stewart's Creek ran close the Old Seal House, and I sometimes fished in the area. On one occasion, I probably dozed off, because all of a sudden, a gaggle of girls were splashing and playing in the creek just around the next bend.

I'd never thought about seeing girls on my creek, and being a bit bashful, I did the only logical thing that came to mind; I grabbed fishing pole and can of worms, and high-tailed back up the creek to where I came from. I hoped and prayed they didn't see me, because the last thing I needed was for somebody find out I ran from a bunch of silly girls.

(In 2011, I stopped by to talk with Lizzie Seal Hawks about her former home place: the Old Seal House. At that time, she was 101 years old and getting around as well as me, if not better. I asked if she even used a cane and she said the hoe was her cane that day.)

When Lizzie's husband Clarence Hawks died, her sister Josie Seal, (who was a year younger) moved in with her. Both attended Zion Hill School and both graduated from the old Beulah School in 1931. (I graduated from the new Beulah School in 1950.)

Lizzie Seal Hawks at age 101 (2011)

The Edgar Smith/Sam and Ella Seal house

Imogene Church Road continued downhill by Sam and Ella Smith Seal's white two-story frame house. It was huge, with many rooms, a tin roof, and was once the home of the Edgar Smith family. (Ella's dad.) When I fished along Sam's bottoms, the house looked like a mansion standing up on the hill.

I didn't know the Seal and Smith families very well in the early years, but I attended school with Sam and Ella's son Troy, and knew their son Wade. Troy later owned a dairy and Wade became a long-distance truck driver, until a bad accident forced him to make a living at doing other things. (When I got my first job in Mt Airy in 1950, I rode to work with Wade and his wife Pat.)

A Family reunion: date unknown

In front: Edgar Smith. From the left: Grace Easter Smith and Ed Smith, Ella and Sam Seal, Hattie and Manuel Easter and Ila and Gid Willey.

Edgar Smith's 70th birthday celebration
at his house in 1942 (Courtesy of Ethel Calloway Smith)

The Thomas Golding/Jim and Monroe Marshall/
Troy and Faye Seal cabin (2011)

Imogene Church Road continued downhill by Sam and Ella's
garden and crossed a small one-lane bridge over Stewart's Creek. Jim
and Monroe Marshal's log cabin was on a hilltop beyond: built by
Thomas Golding in the 1800s. (Troy and Faye Seal now own the house,
and it has been remodeled.)

Jim and Monroe were two of the people we swapped corn
shuckings, barn and house raisings with. Dave Carson lived around the
next curve, and we traded heavy jobs with him also, and sharecropped
his two small bottoms on Stewart's Creek.

Imogene Church Road was the "back-road" Pa and I used when
we drove to Scraptown about 1948. He bought a case of moonshine
from a big rough looking man who lived up on the mountainside. On
the way back, our A-Model's radiator boiled, and I sweated nails all
the way home.

Back on Old Low Gap Road, Ed and Aunt Grace's son Harry and
his wife Lena Edwards Smith lived in a white frame house on top of
the hill past Zion Hill School. Just beyond on the left was another dark
two-story Seal house: the home of Wesley and Virginia Seal. (Troy and
his wife Faye Hiatt Seal later built their home and dairy where the
house once stood.

A drawing of the Wesley Seal Home

Just across the road was another Seal house not quite as old, with a well house on the back porch, and grape vines on the walls. Sam and Ella Seal lived there before they moved to the Edgar Smith house on Imogene Church Road. My Aunt Maude and her husband Allen Seal also lived there before they bought their own place farther down Old Low Gap Road.

My picture of the Parley Golding home

A road right led to Parley and Lula Golding's two-story white frame home out on the ridge. It had the best view of our mountains anywhere around, and an older Parley sat on the front porch and kept an eye on them. (In later years, I painted a picture of the house for their daughter Maude Golding Smith.)

Lula and Parley Golding Courtesy of Judy Marshall Fulda)

Haste' Puckett and family lived a short distance farther along Old Low Gap Road: in an unpainted frame house on the left. One of Haste's sons, Roger, and two of Jessie Puckett's sons drowned (July 3, 1949) in a farm pond accident near where North Surry School was built in later years. (All three are buried side by side at Zion Hill Cemetery on Pine Ridge Road.) Bill and Essie Lowry lived off the road beyond Haste's house and later moved to Slate Mountain east of Mt Airy, where they owned a country store for many years.

One Saturday night around 1940, my family and I attended an all-night dance at the home of Bill and Claudine Puckett, who lived at the intersection of the Lowry Road. After a hard week in the cornfields, people came from all over to dance, listen to music, eat, drink and have a good time. All of the furniture was moved out of the living room to make a dance floor and that's what they did, while pots of chicken stew cooked on the stove, With claw-hammer banjo and fiddle, the musicians played the "old tunes from across the water," while the old, young, and in between ate, drank, and danced the night away. Even those who didn't know how, danced anyway.

The Bill and Claudine Puckett Home (2011)

The whole house shook from the heavy dancing and the drinks flowed freely: everything from "lemonade to lightnin'." Anyone who drank too much took a nap in the backroom with the kids, then woke up and danced some more.

All too soon, the night, the dance, and the good times came to an end. As always, it was the best dance ever, and Fred "Chisel Chin" Cockerham played one last tune on his fiddle to greet the rising sun. Since it was Sunday, everybody went home and fell into bed.

My Aunt Maude and her husband Allen Seal lived just downhill from the Puckett Home. Their house was inside a curve, very close to the road and stayed covered with dust from the traffic that passed by almost in the front door. Their garden was out back, along with several grape vines and apple trees.

Allen was a farmer and the son of Sam Seal Sr. and had several brothers and sisters: William, Luther, Benton, Mary Ann, Oscar, Sam Jr, Sally, Wesley, Elizabeth, (Lizzie) and Josie. His tobacco pack house was across the road and his horse barn was very old and made of logs, with a wood-shingle roof: just like my grandfather's back on Stewart's Creek.

Aunt Maude and Allen with their daughter Estelle
and her daughter Brenda.

Aunt Maude and my mom were good friends, who swapped
Sunday dinners and gossip. When Allen died, (in 1959) Aunt Maude
gave my dad their tractor and things were never again the same at the
old home place. "Gee," "Haa" and "Whoa didn't work like it had with
the horse, but Pa finally worked it out and never went back to the old
ways. Aunt Maude died in 1983.

John and Eliza Puckett and family lived just beyond Aunt Maude's
in a white frame house on the left. Their kids were Ralph, Blossom,
Jimmy, Buck, and Bobby. John later bought the Linc Gardner place,
which included the huge Gardner Woods I almost lived in when
growing up.

Beyond the Puckett home were the homes of Jeff Davis and Sid
Tolbert, and Old Low Gap Road curved left in front of Ray Jones's
home. Their kids were twins named Hurley and Shirley. When the
school bus stopped at the Jones house one day, Dick Jarrell stabbed
Verlon Marshall in the shoulder with a pocketknife. (When Old Low
Gap Road was later paved, it bypassed the Ray Jones and Sid Gardner
homes.)

The Ray Jones House and former Old Low
Gap Road

The road continued past the Sid Gardner, Shepherd Moore homes and the Dock Puckett Road on the left. Just beyond was the Clyde Mooney and Swanson Beamer homes on the right, and the Sam Clement home on the left: the location of today's LL Cultured Marble Company.

Maple Grove Methodist Church (2011)

Maple Grove Methodist Church was beyond Beamer Road, along with Luther Beamer's huge two-story frame house. My dad bought our first horse horse from Luther around 1940, and around 1950, he bought our second car from him: an A Model Ford sedan. (The house is now the location of today's Holder's Used Auto Parts.)

The Luther Beamer Home

"Rambling Roy "Lyons lived in a white frame house on the right and across the road, Racetrack Road turned left to the Mount Airy Racetrack and continued to Highway 89.

One summer Sunday, we rode in the back of John Puckett's pickup to a race at the racetrack. There were no seats or benches, and everybody sat on the hillside and watched cars and motorcycles fly around the track in a huge cloud of dust. Everybody had a good time, especially those who brought their own refreshments in a paper bag.

The fields and pastures and both sides of Highway 89 were jammed with cars and pickups, as well as both sides of Racetrack Road. Lacy Southern made a parachute jump before the race began and tried to land inside the racetrack but landed a quarter-mile away beyond the creek.

The air was full of dust and the smells of fuel and burning motor oil and so much noise it was impossible to hear anything. Every make of car known to mankind raced around the track: so fast I was almost afraid to watch.

A motorcycle wrecked, another came along and ran into it, and its rider was thrown up into the air, hit the ground and didn't move. I figured he was a goner but both riders got up and walked away. It was an exciting day and everybody went home with roaring ears and a good coat of dust.

Many years later, I saw a 1946 racing article about Curtis Turner, who finished last in a field of eighteen cars at the Mount Airy Race Track.

Race Day at the Mt Airy Racetrack in the 1940s

(Courtesy of the Surry County Historical Society)

Back on the Old Low Gap Road, Ulys Southern lived on the right beyond Racetrack Road. His sons were Ed and Joe. Ed and I were school buddies and during the Big War, we spent many happy school hours drawing and hiding secret war maps in Bruton Snuff and Prince Albert tobacco cans. Ed grew up, became a long distance truck driver, built a new brick home at the Southern home place and died there in a farm tractor accident in later years.

Old Low Gap Road continued by the Sam Flippen home, crossed a small bridge and passed the Hobart Linville house on the right at the top of the hill. The road then joined the "new" Low Gap Road. (Highway 89.)

Old Low Gap Road and Highway 89 intersection

Turning right on Highway 89 led to Pine Ridge Shell Service Station a half-mile west. Just up the road was the home of Harl and Beatrice Holder, who were once our neighbors. Turning left on Highway 89 led past Racetrack Road at the bottom of Will Davis Hill and continued to Mount Airy five miles to the east.

The Harl and Beatrice Holder home near
Pine Ridge (2011)

In the early years, traffic was light on Highway 89, but I could usually thumb a ride almost anywhere, because everybody knew everybody and were not afraid to pick up hitchhikers.

Someone said he was thumbing home on Highway 89 and got a ride halfway there. He began thumbing again, but with no cars going his way, he started thumbing the other way and got a ride back to Mount Airy where he started. (As of today, hundreds of cars pass every day: at 80 miles an hour and nobody is about to stop and pick up a hitchhiker.)

Chapter 5
Old Low Gap Road West

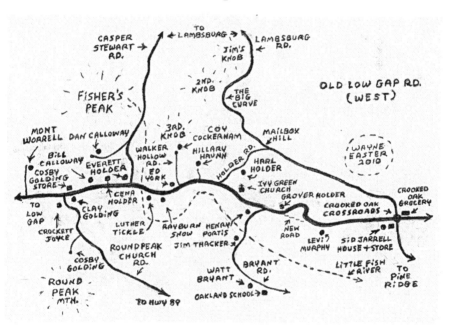

The Crossroads

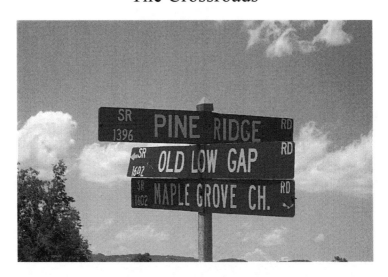

Old Low Gap Road West

Old Low Gap Road West

Sid and Evie Jarrell's home

Sid and Evie Jarrell lived just west of Crooked Oak Cross Roads: in a white two-story house on Old Low Gap Road. (Because of where it led, we called it Round Peak Road.) Sid was a schoolteacher who owned a small store at the crossroads. Their kids were: Oren, Osler, Arlen, Emogene, Bernell, Clellan, and Josie-Faye: all older than me. Osler died in the Big War in 1944.

Sid and Evie Jarrell in the early 1900s, with Sid's two children: (By his first wife) Porter and Lola

(Photo courtesy of Nadine Marshall French)

Levi Murphy and his wife Clemmie lived in a small wooded hollow beyond the Jarrell home. He was a rural mail carrier and come Hell or high water, the mail would be delivered, or else. A road working crew had set some dynamite that was about to explode, when Levi came along. They tried to stop him, but he said nobody was going to stop the US Mail, and drove his horse and buggy on through. He had just cleared the area when the dynamite exploded.

Many years earlier, Old Blind Topsy lived in the same hollow, She was "witched," put hexes on people, cured ailments, removed warts, read signs and caused milk to clabber while still in the cow. It was said she was still out there in the dark and "got" somebody every now and then. (I thought about her quite a bit when going anywhere at night.)

The unpaved Old Low Gap Road continued downhill through some bumpy curves by the Grover Holder home. It was a rough bicycle ride and I kept my tongue well back when riding there, because chattering teeth could make hash out of it. Someone said he tied a fertilizer sack on the back of his car to catch all the parts that fell off there.

The Grover Holder home place today

The Grover Holder farm was huge: with several tobacco barns and huge bottoms. The family lived in a white frame house in a curve at the bottom of the hill. The kids were: Aldine, Gaynell, James, Wayne, Colin, and Linda. The road originally curved around up a small valley and came back near the mobile home seen in the photo.

(I was repairing Grover's t v antenna in later years, fell off his house and just missed a well top in the back yard. I looked around to see if anybody was watching, and since nobody was there to offer sympathy, I climbed back on the house and went back to work.)

Bryant Road branched left off Old Low Gap Road and led by Grover's rental house near Little Fish River. Henry Portis and family lived there and their kids were Joe, Jack, Glenn, Tom and Alice. Tom and I worked together at what we called "The Plastic Plant" in the 1950s. Jack died in a fiery gas tanker wreck on an icy Highway 52 between Mount Airy and Pilot Mountain. (December 27, 1983.)

Bryant Road then crossed Little Fish River, (near where Greenwood's Mill stood in earlier times) and climbed Thacker's Knob by Jim Thacker's home. Like most of our country dirt roads, it was bumpy and a steep uphill push for a bicycle.

The Watt and Ada Bryant home

Bryant Road was named for Watt Bryant who lived on top of Thacker Knob. His wife Addie was Jim Smith's daughter and after Jim's wife Carrie died, he lived with Watt and family. Their children were Porter, Weldon, Frances, Alice, Joe, and Aaron Brintle, (son of Addie and her first husband.)

Watt's water system was system similar to William Senter's on Easy Street, and he wound water along a cable that ran over the road to the spring down in the valley. (I learned about it when a bucket of water went by overhead.)

Oakland School once stood on the right beyond Watt's house: one of the two schools Mama attended in the 1920s. Bryant Road continued to Round Peak Church Road and Shipp's Mustering Ground where Revolutionary war veterans met for annual reunions in the 1820s. Hardin "Skittt" Talliaferro, who grew up along Little Fish River, wrote about the meetings in his book "Fisher's River Scenes."

Ivy Green Church

Continuing along Old Low Gap Road, Ivy Green Church stood on the hilltop above the Grover Holder home. It was a white two-story building when I was growing up, but was later covered with bricks and expanded. (Many of our former friends and neighbors are buried in the church cemetery.)

Except for foot washings and funerals, my family didn't go to church, although members of several churches invited us. A preacher once told us he was making a "Christian Endeavor" to persuade people to go to his new church. According to him, if we didn't do so, we would burn in the fiery furnaces of Hell. We didn't go to his church either.

Warren and I broke tradition when free bags of candy and oranges were given away at a play at Ivy Green at Christmas. We decided maybe churches were o k after all.

Round Peak Masonic Lodge met upstairs in the two-story building, and supposedly, they had a mean guard goat. "Don't you boys even think about going up there." They later built a new one-story lodge across the road, and I wondered where they kept the goat.

A no-longer used road led downhill through a wooded area behind the church, crossed Holder Road and followed a ridge back into a valley where one-legged "Big Sid" Marshall once lived. The only remains of his home were some chimney rocks and a few flowers and red bud trees that bloomed in spring.

Continuing along Old Low Gap Road, Holder Road (later named Tony Holder Road) turned right and led over and down what we called Ivy Green Hill, then through Harl Holder's huge farm, and back to Mailbox Hill on Lambsburg Road.

Tommy Jarrell (of Round Peak Music fame) and many of his kin people grew up near the Old Low Gap/Holder Road intersection and Jarrell's Store and Round Peak Post Office were once located there. (All were long-gone by the 1940s.)

The Hillary and Ada Haunn House

At the bottom of the hill, Little Fish River meandered along beside Old Low Gap Road, where a driveway on the right climbed the hill to the white-frame home of Hillary and Ada Marshall Haunn. (Most locals called them "The Hornes.") Ada was Walter and Oscar Marshall's sister and their children were Carlos, Eliza, Guy, Columbus, Helen and Roger.

They owned a huge farm, grew corn and tobacco and Guy and Pa sometimes made moonshine. Their "nursery bought" black walnut tree grew walnuts twice as big the wild walnuts that grew on Stewart's Creek.

91

Hillary and Ada Marshall Haunn

One Saturday night in the 1950s, their son Columbus, myself, and some other young men of the world were riding around in my first car: drinking moonshine and acting like grownups.

We were floating about three feet off the ground when Columbus decided to go home. He wouldn't let me drive him up to the house, but sat down by their mailbox to rest: with his half-full fruit jar beside him. He didn't rest very long, because just as we drove off, we met a state trooper, who stopped at the mailbox beside Columbus.

We eased on over the road just like we were living at the foot of the cross. Being in the wee hours of Sunday morning, we were probably getting a head start on Sunday school.) Lucky for us, the trooper didn't chase us down, but he arrested Columbus.

Coy Cockerham and family lived at the end of Walker's Hollow Road, located beyond the Haunn place. My family and I attended another all-night square dance there on another Saturday night. A crowd of people gathered in, made music and danced into the wee hours of the morning. Unlike the dance at Bill Puckett's home, we left early. (I think my parents were getting older.)

Old Low Gap Road continued by the Rayburn Snow and Luther Tickle homes and crossed Little Fish River near the intersection of what later became The Casper Stewart Road that ran between Round Peak and Lambsburg.

The Everette Holder home in 2011

Everette Holder and family lived at the intersection in a white frame house at the foot of Fisher's Peak. In October 1975, hang gliders launched from Bald Rock on top of the peak, sailed around for very long time, then landed in Everette's pasture.

The Bill Calloway home (2011)

A half-mile past the Cena Holder and Bill Calloway homes, stood Cosby Golding's small country store on the right side of the road. A hand-operated gas pump under the shelter had a handle to pull back and forth that pumped gas into a glass container at the top. It measured the gallons and when the desired amount of gas was pumped, a hose drained it into the car's tank.

Cosby Golding's Store in 1999

On Saturday afternoons, people from all over gathered there to take a break from the mines. One memorable Saturday in the 1940s, Pa and I fired up our A-Model and headed for Round Peak and we too took a break from the cornfield mines.

The joint was already jumping, but Pa knew his game well, and caught up in almost no time. The place was full of bicycles, cars, and pick-ups, with a mule tied to a shade tree. A red-hot poker game was going on out back, people pitched horseshoes, and the moonshine, beer, and R C Colas flowed freely.

The jukebox played a song called "Jody Blonde: so loud it could've been heard by a deaf person five miles away. Everybody was everybody's friend and the sawmill workers, who had the most money, played the most poker, had the most fun and probably didn't get out of bed next day, or maybe the next, for that matter. Late in the day, Pa and I headed back down the road toward Jim's Knob and home.

In later years, I took my own breaks there, but there was never another Saturday afternoon like that first one at Cosby Golding's Store in Round Peak.

Just beyond Cosby's Store, Round Peak Church Road branched left, climbed Round Peak Mountain and continued to Highway 89 at Charles Snow's Oak Grove Grocery.

On another Saturday night, my pals and I were again riding around in my first car. I don't remember what we celebrated, but come Sunday morning, we woke up stuck in a side ditch on Lundy Hill: about half way along Round Peak Church Road between Cosby's Store and Highway 89. The car's clutch and transmission were ruined, the fenders were bent and one of the tires was flat. Nobody remembered what happened, but somebody said we probably had too much to drink. The car was beyond repair!

On another Saturday afternoon, another car load of us stopped at Carl Nunn's beer joint on Highway 89 to re-stock the trunk of my second car: a 1940 Olds. We were already "two sheets in the wind, when somebody suggested we go to a dance in Galax Virginia. Doing my usual terrific job of driving while drinking, we actually made it a a mile before we crashed in a deep gully just past Round Peak Church Road. Everybody landed on their faces, but nobody was seriously hurt.

For the second time, my car was beyond repair, and my driver's license was revoked for a year. Soon after, Uncle Sam came calling; I was drafted into the army and had no driver's license for the next two years. I learned my lesson slowly, but I learned it well; never again did I drink and drive.

My 1940 Oldsmobile

The Mont Worrell Home

Beyond Round Peak Church Road, Old Low Gap Road continued by the home of Mont Worrell, who lived on a hillside at the foot of Fisher's Peak. I knew many other people in the Round Peak area, but knew Mont Worrell best of all. He was our Route 1 Low Gap N C mail carrier and on occasion, I met him at the mailbox every day to see if my order came. (He later moved to Mt Airy and built a new brick home on Highway 89.) Old Low Gap Road continued west to the village of Low Gap, five miles away.

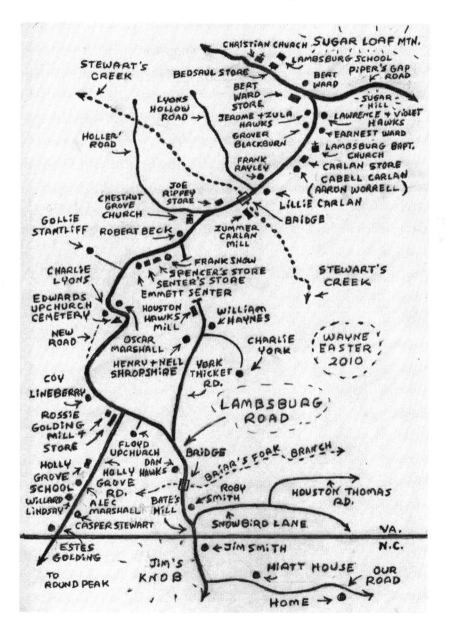

Bate's Hill
at the North Carolina/Virginia state line on Lambsburg Road

Road to Lambsburg

Our home on Banjo Lane (1955)

One day around 1940, Grandpa came by our house in his one-horse wagon, headed for Rossie Golding's mill on Lambsburg Road. We loaded *our* sack of corn and my bucket of blackberries into the wagon and headed for Virginia on my first big business trip.

My drawing of the Hiatt House

We rode uphill by a one-room log cabin we called the Hiatt House: named for Alfred Hiatt who once lived there. I was born there in 1932, as my dad said it, "On the windiest damn ridge I ever seen."

Jim's Knob stood just to the west, and a road across the valley climbed over a hill to Houston Thomas's home on Stewart's Creek. Three miles away in the background stood Sugar Loaf Mountain at Lambsburg.

At the foot of Jim's Knob, we turned right onto Lambsburg Road by Jim and Carrrie Smith's two-room log cabin, which was surrounded by grape vines. Jim sold homemade wine, and neighbors gathered in on Saturday nights to listen to the Grand Old Opry on their battery powered radio: the first in our country.

As we crossed the state line and started down Bate's Hill, the wagon began to shake, rattle, and roll on the rocky road. (The Virginia D O T kept their unpaved roads covered with crushed rock to help fight mud in winter, but it didn't work well on Bates Hill.

Roby Smith and family lived in a log cabin on Bates Hill: beside Bluebird Lane, which led back to the homes of Farley Smith and Little Sid Marshall. A spring path led downhill from the house, crossed Lambsburg Road and continued to their spring at the foot of Jim's Knob. Like ours, it was worn deep from carrying water along it for many years.

As we rolled down the steepest part of Bate's Hill, Grandpa rode the brake stick with his foot to keep the wagon from running over the horse. (The brake pad was a piece of an old automobile tire that rubbed against the metal wheel rims.)

The wheel noise slacked off as we crossed the one-lane bridge over Briar's Fork Branch. Since it began in the mountain above Casper Stewart's home, I called it "Stewart's Branch." It fell out of the mountain, crossed Holly Grove Road, wandered along through Lyons's pasture, continued by the north side of Jim's Knob, and crossed Lambsburg Road.

Under the bridge was a great place to get out of the hot sun in mid-summer and no kid could pass by without checking it out. It took a certain amount of wading and rock throwing to keep the branch running anyway and I tried to do my part. It was also a handy place to re-fill boiling radiators, horses, mules and people. When a car drove by overhead, the bridge shook like it would fall.

While on the way to Rossie's mill another day, I stopped to check under the bridge, while my sack of corn rested on a rock, I waded downstream and the fun began: horny-heads were building nests in the underwater gravel and I found a dead catfish lying on a sandbar.

There were so many great things to see, I forgot all about the time and waded all the way to Stewart's Creek. I got back home late in the day, and Mama asked me, "Where you been all day and what mill did you go to? I coulda' crawled there and back before now."

Lambsburg Road continued up-hill by Dan Hawk's two-story house on the left. We once sharecropped his fields, and his son Elmer went away to the Big War in the 1940s, and was never heard from again. Dan later shot himself on the front porch of the house and when his farm was sold at auction, I bought a can of used nails for ten cents.

When Grandpa and I drove around a curve beyond York Thicket Road, the Blue Ridge Mountain hung high overhead: all the way from Fisher's Peak to the Sugar Loaf at Lambsburg. Floyd Upchurch's home and barn were downhill on the left, and I could see the Three Knobs west of our house.

Rossie Golding's Store

Rossie Golding's Store was at the intersection of Lambsburg and Holly Grove Roads: a one-story frame building with a tin roof. He and his wife Inez lived in one end of the building, and the store was in the other. Since we almost never had money, we traded them eggs, blackberries and stuff we grew on the farm, for coffee, sugar and stuff we couldn't grow on the farm.

Rossie Golding's Mill

Rossie's mill was in a ram-shackle building behind the store and powered by an old automobile engine. He pulled on a belt to crank the engine, and the air was instantly filled with flapping belts, smoke, meal dust and noise, and a white coat of meal dust covered everything, including Rossie. So much was happening, it was impossible to keep up.

He poured shelled corn into a hopper that vibrated, and kept the corn feeding down into the mill. The meal finally came out of a chute at the bottom; Rossie kept part of it to pay for the grinding and dipped the rest into our flour sacks. I sold him my bucket of blackberries and spent all the money for candy. (A paper poke full of all-day suckers was almost as good as Christmas.)

We loaded everything in the wagon, untied the horse and headed back down the rocky road toward Jim's Knob and home: knowing we would not go hungry any time soon. (That was our only wagon trip together.)

Holly Grove Road branched off Lambsburg Road at Rossie's store, passed by Holly Grove School and continued to Round Peak. I knew all of the kids who attended the school in the 1940s, and my family and I attended a "Cake Walk" fund-raiser there. The couples danced in a circle, then stopped on a number and the two whose number was pulled from a hat won a cake. (I don't remember eating any of the cakes.) The building later became Holly Grove Church.

Holly Grove Church, formerly Holly Grove School

Aus Lyons, who lived beside to the school, sold used clothing and I bought a worn-out black-leather jacket there for fifty cents. It was too big, but after a few coats of black shoe polish and some elbow grease, it almost looked good. Mr. Cool then wore it to school and impressed all the girls.

Willard Lindsay, who also lived on Holly Grove Road, was a lucky man; he owned a buckeye tree. By carrying a buckeye in your pocket, you'd have the best of luck. I sometimes carried two, because you could never have too much good luck.

Casper Stewart and family lived on a hillside beyond the Lindsay place. He was a photographer who made family portraits all around the country. In the late 1930s, he made photos of my family, my grandparents, and the Jim Smith and Walter Marshall families.

Beyond the Stewart home, Estes Golding lived at the state line in the last house on the right in Virginia. After crossing the state line, Holly Grove Road became Casper Stewart Road.

One day in late 1948, Pa and I headed for Lambsburg in our A-Model. I was trying out my brand new driver's license, and doing a first rate job, until we met a car going almost too fast to see: exactly in front of Rossie's Mill.

I looked out the back window to see where it went and wandered over to the left side of the road. That's when the second car came along going just as fast, and to avoid hitting us, it ran out of the road and crashed under Rossie's woodpile.

103

A Blue Ridge Parkway Ranger crawled out of the wreck, threw his hat on the ground and said, "Why in the name of Heaven don't you stay on your side of the road. When I told him we were about of control, he agreed. (He said he was chasing a load of moonshine from off the Parkway.)

Lambsburg Road continued by the home of Coy Lineberry, who lived in a house Rossie originally built for his mother when she got older. The road continued around the foot of Sam's Knob, circled around Edwards-Upchurch Cemetery, and passed by the home of Charlie Lyons. (The curve was bypassed in later years.)

The Oscar and Lillie Marshall home

Oscar and Lilly Marshall and family lived in a white frame house just down the hill. Their kids were Alec, Gertrude, Betty Jo, James, Joyce, Mary, Benton, Ruth, Rachael, Janette, and Fred.

They had moved there from our area when I was still young, but still owned the Old, New, and Hiatt houses near us. I ran wild in their huge woods as I grew up: hunting and fishing, and we sharecropped their bottoms on Stewart's Creek, and lived in their "New House" for a year.

Their son Alec was co-owner of Shelton Plumbing in Mt Airy, and was everybody's friend. He gave people free advice about their plumbing problems, and saved my "do-it-yourself-hide" several times over the years. He and his wife lived on Holly Grove Road beyond Holly Grove School.

Just beyond the Marshalls lived Golly Stantliff, back off the road: with a whole mountain in his yard. (We pronounced his last name "Stanley.") He was an auctioneer who rode the back roads with a record player and loudspeaker on his car: playing gospel music

When he came through our country one day, I thought the Angels were singing in the sky and it scared me out of my wits. Record player or no record player, I was never quite sure he wasn't in cahoots with somebody "up-there."

Hurley and Rachael Smith lived on Log Cabin Lane across from the Stantliff Road. He was born in the log cabin Hiatt House in 1922: some ten years before me. He was a saw-miller and hunter, and like my dad, made moonshine.

Senter's Store

Continuing on Lambsburg Road, Emmett Senter owned Senter's Store beside his house, and the Frank Snow home and Spencer's small store were on the right beyond.

York Thicket Road turned right at the bottom of the hill, and led by Houston Hawks's Mill and woodworking shop. He made furniture and cane-back chairs, and in later years the Mt. Airy Museum displayed a large photo of him making a chair.

York Thicket Road continued by the homes of William and Ethel Haynes, Carlyle and Nell Shropshire Stanley, Charlie and Mayzie York, and back into Lambsburg Road near the Dan Hawks place. Carlyle and Nell once ran a small store from the back of their house.

Robert Beck and family lived beyond York Thicket Road, directly behind Chestnut Grove Primitive Baptist Church. The church was established June 1902, and faced Sugar Loaf Mountain: with Fisher's Peak out back.

Just like at Crooked Oak Church on Pine Ridge Road, Foot-washing Day came every summer at Chestnut Grove: with lemonade, ice cream and huge tables of fried chicken and every kind of food known to mankind. For at least two days a year, I ate well, very well.

On weekends, local men and boys parked their cars, trucks, bicycles, horses and mules under shade trees beside the cemetery, made music, drank moonshine and beer, and played poker.

The single men and boys watched the neighborhood girls walk by on Lambsburg Road, and the married men watched the seasons change on Sugar Loaf Mountain across the valley. I was there every chance I got and my pals Wayne Golding, Albert Upchurch and Darrel Hawks and I tried to do our part.

Chestnut Grove Primitive Baptist Church (Est. June 1902)

The original church building was later moved across the road beside the cemetery and a new brick church was built where the old one stood. Just as in days gone by, people still loafed beside the cemetery on weekends: watched the girls go by and kept an eye on Sugar Loaf Mountain.

The "Holler' Road" (today's Parkwood Lane) intersection was just below the church and just down the road stood Joe Rippey's small country store. (In the late 1930s, people gathered at Jim Smith's house

106

on Saturday nights to listen to the Grand Old Opry on his battery powered radio.) In the early 1950s, people gathered at Joe Rippey's Store to watch the Saturday Night Fights on a new-fangled thing called television.

The t v sat on a high shelf, so everybody could watch the fights, while they ate Moon Pies and drank Nehi 'sody-pop and R C Colas. On occasion, moonshine was passed around outside, and on occasion, a real fight broke out in the parking lot. Then, everybody gathered outside, and everybody agreed: the outside fights were better than the inside fights.

Joe Rippey's Store building (2008)

On summer weekends, a barnstorming pilot landed his small plane across the road and sold $5.00 rides. Since I'd been big enough to see a plane, I'd wanted to ride and had real dreams of an airplane falling out of the sky: right on top of me. (When Jerome Faulkner and the pilot did a tailspin one day, I thought the dream was coming true.)

With almost my last cent, I took a ride and it was an eye-opener; the plane shook, rattled, and vibrated so bad, a blind person could see we had a major emergency on hand. The fact that there was nothing but a little bit of airplane between the seat of my pants and the ground made matters even worse. I knew for a fact, the plane was about to fly all to pieces.

The pilot didn't seem worried about crashing and burning, and when my heart finally settled down, I decided maybe it wasn't so bad after all. In a very short time, it was the greatest thing that ever happened, even better than I'd thought it would be.

From high in the sky, I could see every fishing hole on Stewart's Creek and all the fields we hoed corn in. We flew over our house and Mama waved from the yard. We flew over Jim's Knob, Round Peak, and Fisher's Peak and it was an unforgettable day. There were other plane rides in later years, but none as exciting as that first one I made from a cow pasture at Joe Rippey's Store.

While landing one day, a wheel assembly broke, the plane flipped around and stopped with one end of the wing on the ground. There was almost no damage, but the pilot said if it had happened on takeoff, it could've been serious. I didn't ride that day!

(Joe Rippey's Store eventually closed, and the building became a residence. In 2009, it was demolished, and a new home was built on the same spot, where so many cars and so many people gathered on Saturday nights so many years ago.)

Zummer Carlan's huge turbine gristmill once stood at the bottom of the hill: on the south side of Stewart's Creek. I never met Zummer, but I remember being on the bridge the late 1930s, and seeing the dark building.

The whole community gathered there and and people came from miles away to loaf, tell tall tales, and have their corn and other grains ground into flour and meal and trade at the store.

A millrace high over Lambsburg Road brought water from a dam upstream that powered the mill. Neighborhood Kids played under the continually dripping millrace in summer and the drips became icicles in winter.

Beyond the creek, Lambsburg Road continued by Lillie Carlan's small house on the right, the Frank Rayley house stood on a bank above the road. Just beyond, Aaron Worrell lived in a huge white house on the right. Aaron's brother Mont Worrell was our Route 1, Low Gap N C mail carrier for many years. The Carlan family (of Carlan's Mill) originally built the house, along with a huge feed barn and a store that stood beside it.

Lambsburg Baptist Church and the Earnest Ward Home were just past the Worrell home: backed up against Sugar Hill, and just beyond were the homes of Grover Blackburn and Lawrence Hawks.

The Aaron Worrell/Cabell Carlan home

Lambsburg Baptist Church (2011)

Grover Blackburn's home

109

The Lawrence and Violet Hawks home (2011)

The Jerome and Zula Hawks home (2011)

The last house on the left on Lambsburg Road was the home of Jerome and Zula Hawks. Zula wrote a book, "Memory Springs" that described the area, the people and their springs, as she remembered them from growing up in and around Lambsburg.

She wrote about Foot Washing Days at Chestnut Grove Church, living at the Bob Faulkner place on Dobson (Lambsburg) Road in North Carolina about 1910, and living in the John Bates log cabin in winter. She wrote about attending Holly Grove School and all of the people and places she once knew.

The intersection of Lambsburg and
Piper's Cap Roads (2011)

Just beyond the Hawks home, Lambsburg Road joined Piper's
Gap Road in the shadow of Sugar Loaf Mountain. Turning left led by
the Bert Ward home on the right, and his store across the road on the
left. I remember him buying blackberries, as Rossie Golding did at his
Store.

Bert Ward's home (2011)

Bert Ward's Store in Lambsburg
(Courtesy of Bernelle Ward Holder)

Woodrow Bedsaul's Store building (2011)

Woodrow Bedsaul's Store and post office were farther up the street, along with Lambsburg School and Lambsburg Christian Church. I knew quite a few people who lived in that part of Lambsburg, including the Wards, Hawks, Lambs, and Bedsaul families, but not as well as those who lived "Up the Holler."

When I first began driving, I cleaned out the side-ditches in downtown Lambsburg, and became well acquainted with Virginia State Troopers. Everybody on Main Street knew me, including the state troopers and deputy sheriffs. Anytime I met either, they searched my car, but whatever they were hunting for, they never found. (Actually, I was really a pretty straight character and Pa only had to go to Hillsville once to keep me out of jail.)

The Old Lambsburg School building

The New Lambsburg School (2011)

Lambsburg Christian Church (2011)

Piper's Gap Road continued up the mountain through Bobbitt Holler' to Galax Virginia. Pa said our worst winter storms came "straight outtta' Bobbitt Holler', which we could see from our house.

We lived three miles away and during summer dry spells, we could see rain falling in Bobbitt Holler: when we didn't get a drop. Pa said it rained there when it rained nowhere else in the world, because they paid the preacher better than we did.

Chapter 7
Road to Stewart's Creek

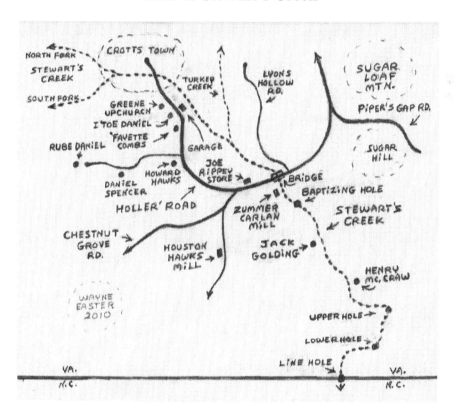

NORTH FORK
STEWART'S
CREEK

SOUTH FORK

CROTTS TOWN

TURKEY
CREEK

LYONS
HOLLOW
RD.

SUGAR
LOAF
MTN.

PIPER'S GAP RD.

GREENE
UPCHURCH

I TOE DANIEL

FAVETTE
COMBS

RUBE DANIEL

GARAGE

SUGAR
HILL

DANIEL
SPENCER

HOWARD
HAWKS

JOE
RIPPEY
STORE

BRIDGE

BAPTIZING HOLE

HOLLER' ROAD

ZUMMER
CARLAN
MILL

STEWART'S
CREEK

CHESTNUT
GROVE
RD.

HOUSTON
HAWKS
MILL

JACK
GOLDING

HENRY
MC. CRAW

WAYNE
EASTER
2010

UPPER HOLE

LOWER HOLE

LINE HOLE

VA.
N.C.

VA.
N.C.

Stewart's Creek at Lambsburg

Road to Stewart's Creek

A million years ago, give or take a few, Stewart's Creek began as two different streams on top of the Blue Ridge Mountain. After long downhill journeys, both splashed out into an area now called Crotts Town, joined together and continued along a valley called The Holler.' (Today's Parkwood Lane.)

In the late 1800s, Lewis and Celia Crotts moved to the area, hewed a cherry orchard from the mountainside and raised a family. Around 1940, their grandson Bud, hand-dug our new well, and to avoid two long walks each day, he slept in our barn overnight. Thanks to his man-killing work, we no longer toted water up a steep hill.

I knew the Holler' area of Lambsburg best of all, because most people who lived there either farmed, worked at sawmills or both and all lived close to the land, just like my family. Their cornfields were the "darkest green ever seen:" almost as black as the ground they grew in. The Indians fared well there too, because there were arrowheads everywhere in the bottoms in the early years. .

It took a brave soul to go swimming in Stewart's Creek in the middle of winter, but being true mountaineers, "them Up-the-Holler people" backed off from nothing or nobody." Every year on New Year's Eve, some of the bravest got all moonshined-up," and brought in the New Year by skinny-dipping in the ice-cold creek at midnight. Just thinking about it froze my socks off. With a huge bon fire and moonshine waiting on the bank, nobody froze to death.

Almost everybody, including a few girls, hunted bee trees, set rabbit gums, and fished in Stewart's Creek. They hunted squirrels in mountainsides so steep, they couldn't see the sky unless they leaned far over backwards. That could be life threatening, because anyone who leaned too far back fell out of the mountain and got "all stoved up and weren't no good for nothing or nobody nevermore, ever."

I was told (by a very reliable source, of course) that a good "Up the Holler" man had no need to climb the mountain to go squirrel hunting. He just stood on his back porch, shot a squirrel in a tree high in the mountain, and caught it in a fertilizer sack when it fell out of the sky. I was never lucky enough to see it done, but as my reliable source swore on a stack of Bibles, "Boy, them Up the Holler' people don't tell no lies about nothing."

Another truthful soul said when an apple fell off a tree; they just held a fertilizer sack open at the bottom of the mountain and caught it when it came bouncing down the hill. Once again, I was never lucky enough to see it happen.

According to Old Timers, people once "made wages by panning for gold in the sandbars of Stewart's Creek and rumors were told of saddlebags of Confederate gold: hidden and lost under a hanging rock somewhere in Lambsburg Mountain.

I made a one-time trip there to check out my scouting abilities and treasure hunting techniques. Someone said he didn't remember why he quit wearing boots until he tried wearing another pair. About halfway up the mountain, I remembered why I'd only climbed Fisher's Peak once. (I finally made it up the mountain, but to the best of my knowledge, the gold is still there.)

A drawing of the Greene Upchurch home

The Upchurch family came to the Crotts Town area from Wilkes County, N C around the turn of the century. Green and Sarah built a log cabin up the Holler' and raised a family. Their six children were: Lessie, Jack, Dennis, Warren, Emma, and Early. (As of today, Dennis is the only survivor; he is one hundred years of age and the Upchurch cabin still stands near Stewart's Creek.)

Greene and Sarah Upchurch

Howard and Emma Upchurch Williams

(Howard and Emma Upchurch Williams (daughter of Greene and Sarah) were my wife Helen's parents. Emma died in 1950 and Howard died in 1961.

I-Toe (Otto) Daniel and his wife Cartie lived just down Holler' Road from the Greene Upchurch home. He was a mechanic who had a one-bay garage at his house. In the early 1950s, he overhauled the engine in my first car: a 1939 Plymouth coupe that seen a hard life. The car then ran like new until some pals and I woke up one Sunday morning wrecked in a side ditch on Lundy Hill in Round Peak.

I-Toe's Garage

Hurley Smith and I-Toe Daniel (Around 1950)
(Courtesy of the late Rachel Senter Smith)

Stewart's Creek continued downstream down by the Lafayette "Fayette" Combs and Howard Hawks homes. Howard was a rural mail carrier, and sold my dad our first car in 1948: an A-Model coupe he had used on the mail route.

The Howard Hawks home

Turkey Creek began near the Blue Ridge Parkway on top of Piper's Gap Mountain, splashed downhill west of Bobbitt Holler and joined Stewart's Creek in Lyons Hollow: just west of the bridge on Lambsburg Road.

Zummer Carlan's water-powered turbine mill once stood just below the bridge on the south side of Stewart's Creek. People brought corn and other grains from miles away to be ground into the staffs of life: meal and flour. Zummer kept a small part of it as payment and traded coffee, sugar and canned goods for farm produce.

An August 1940 hurricane brought what became known as the Forty Flood, and the old timers said it was "worser than than'that'n in 1916." The mill and the bridge were totally destroyed and pieces of both, along with canned goods, were found in the ruined fields far downstream. It was like Christmas for local kids and some grownups, as they hunted the lost merchandise. A new bridge was built just above where the old one stood, but the mill was never replaced.

By then, water-powered mills were already relics of the past, and Houston Hawks and Rossie Golding both had the new type: powered by an automobile engine. Every family in our area had their corn ground into meal at one of the two mills. Rossie's Mill was closest and our favorite, because distance was important when totin' a sack of shelled corn along the rocky road barefooted.

Zummer Carlan's Mill
Shown left to right: Geneva Snow Stockwell, Julia Snow Williams, and Frances Snow Wilmar. (Photo courtesy of the late Dorothy Ward Taylor.)

Pa told of a Lambsburg man who "went away to work," bought a new "suit of clothes" and a new motorcycle. He came back home "all dressed up in style", and was riding around seeing and being seen. He wrecked in a mud hole across the creek from Carlan's Mill, and the motorcycle landed on top of him: still running. After it churned him up and down in the mud a while, he got back on it, rode out of town and never came back.

When revivals were held at local churches and someone got saved; they were baptized in a fishing hole below the bridge. On Baptizing Day, a crowd gathered to watch the preacher and a helper dunk the saved people under water, which "got all the meanness out." One day someone yelled at the preacher, "You'd better dunk that'n two or three times, Preach', 'cause he's got a whole lot 'a meanness in him."

Stewart's Creek continued southeast, where the bottoms became larger than those up the Holler'. Bottoms were the best land of all and those who owned them lived a little higher up the social ladder than us dry-ridge farmers. Even in drought years, corn grew well in bottoms, unless a flood washed it away.

The Henry and Callie McCraw home

Stewart's Creek turned away from the mountain, and ran by the Creed and Jack Golding farms on the north side of area we called "No Man's Land." What I called Stewart's Branch crossed Lambsburg Road at the foot of Jim's Knob, and joined Stewart's Creek near Henry McCraw's home. From there, all the way to Dave Carson's Big Bottom in North Carolina, Stewart's Creek was almost mine, because I almost never saw anyone else while fishing and prowling in the area.

From high in the sky, Sugar Loaf Mountain kept watch over "my country," as buzzards floating in the sky became eagles flying over the "Great North Woods. Squirrels thrashing in the hillside hickory trees became wild painters (panthers) on their way to the mountain: riding a treetop highway. A tall dead lightning struck tree stood in the hillside, just waiting for the eagles to come home.

Huge splashes around the next bend told me there were whales to be caught and arrowheads in McCraw's bottoms proved the Indians once lived there. The whole creek was catfish heaven, and the very best fishing was always in the next hole just around the next bend. With a tin can of worms, a fishing pole, .22 rifle, Barlow knife, and telescope, I was prepared and this scout was there every chance he got.

McCraw's two fishing holes were great places to fish, but only when the creek was muddy. Even then, I never caught any of the whoppers I'd heard splashing. Just like the rabbits I tried to track in the snow, fish were smarter than me.

The North Carolina-Virginia state line crossed Stewart's Creek at the Line Hole, just below McCraw's fishing holes. I didn't know exactly where the state line was, but I sat on a rock in Virginia and hoped I was fishing in North Carolina.

The Line Hole (2009)

A barbed wire fence crossed Stewart's Creek at the Line Hole. A broken-off fence post was still attached to the wire and as the creek flowed under it, it was lifted out of the water and fell back in: making a continual splashing sound. (A few days later, the wire was still there, but the post was gone.)

I sat at the Line Hole one early spring day, and watched white clouds draw ever-changing pictures in a deep blue sky. New grass was growing and the blackberry vines had new leaves. Maples bloomed red in the hillsides and a lookout crow called from the top of a pine tree. It was great to know winter was finally gone, and I hoped to be there fishing, every single day, all summer long.

Chapter 8
Road to the End

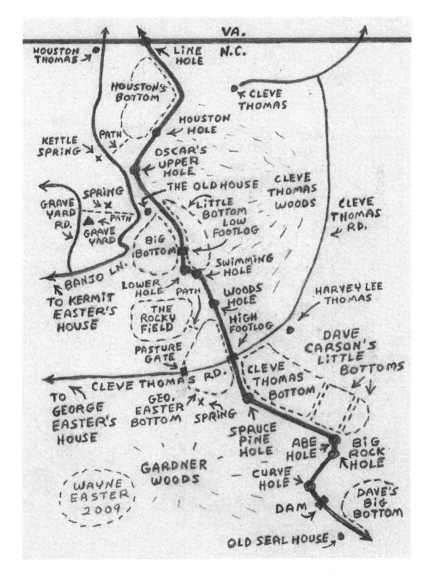

VA.

N.C.

HOUSTON THOMAS

LINE HOLE

HOUSTON'S BOTTOM

CLEVE THOMAS

HOUSTON HOLE

PATH

KETTLE SPRING

OSCAR'S UPPER HOLE

THE OLD HOUSE

CLEVE THOMAS WOODS

CLEVE THOMAS RD.

SPRING

LITTLE BOTTOM

GRAVE YARD RD.

PATH

GRAVE YARD

LOW FOOTLOG

BIG BOTTOM

SWIMMING HOLE

BANJO LN.

LOWER HOLE

PATH

WOODS HOLE

HARVEY LEE THOMAS

TO KERMIT EASTER'S HOUSE

THE ROCKY FIELD

HIGH FOOTLOG

DAVE CARSON'S LITTLE BOTTOMS

PASTURE GATE

CLEVE THOMAS RD.

CLEVE THOMAS BOTTOM

TO GEORGE EASTER'S HOUSE

GEO. EASTER BOTTOM

SPRING

SPRUCE PINE HOLE

ABE HOLE

BIG ROCK HOLE

WAYNE EASTER 2009

GARDNER WOODS

CURVE HOLE

DAM

DAVE'S BIG BOTTOM

OLD SEAL HOUSE

Road to the End

The Houston Thomas Bottom: looking upstream in 1971.
(The North Carolina/Virginia state line crossed Stewart's Creek at the tallest trees at center.)

The Houston Thomas bottom (just below the Line Hole) was one of the few we never sharecropped along that part of Stewart's Creek, the main reason being, it was never available for sharecropping. Even so, we made use of it.

When deep winter diets of cornbread, pinto beans and fatback became old, everybody craved something new and green to eat. Beginning in late February, every family in our part of the country headed for last year's cornfields to gather their first mess of the first new green food of the year: creecies.

They were small flat-on-the ground plants that lagged along all winter, then began growing faster. They grew well in last year's cornfields, and no landowner cared who picked his creecies. No matter whose land they were on, they belonged to whoever got there first, and we made the most of it, every year in Houston Thomas's Bottom.

We then had cornbread, pinto beans, fatback, and *creecies* for supper, and grew "fat and sassy again." In fall of the year, we gathered walnuts from a tree in the middle of the bottom. Walnuts grew everywhere along the creek, but Houston's walnuts were the biggest and the best.

The Houston Thomas house

Houston and Zora Ward Thomas's white frame house stood 200 feet south of the Virginia state line: beside the road to our house. (Our road.) It overlooked Stewart's Creek down in the valley: which was the property dividing line between Houston's and the Cleve Thomas places. I don't remember Houston, who died of a heart attack in 1938, but he was a barber who cut hair for neighborhood families, including mine.

Houston's well was so deep it took forever to wind up a bucket of water. I dropped a small rock down inside, and thought it would never hit bottom; when it did, it echoed for a very long time.

Just out from the house was Houston's barn: with a wooden plank corral around it that made it look like what I thought a ranch would look like; all it needed was a chuck wagon, a bunkhouse, some horses and cowboys.

One Saturday night, Avon and Russell Marshall, my brother Warren and I made a nighttime fishing expedition along the creek at Houston's Bottom. We worked out all the details, gathered Pa's lantern, a pocket full of matches, fishing poles, cans of worms, a frying pan, and headed for the great outdoors.

We fought blackberry briars and mosquitoes, chased each other in the dark for hours, and finally caught a few small catfish. We had no watch to tell time, but we checked the moon, the stars and the wind direction, decided the hour was getting late, and climbed the hill to Houston's house.

Our big plan was to sleep n the porch of the then-empty house, (where the snakes couldn't get us) get up in the morning and cook a real campfire breakfast. Since we'd had a hard day, and since everybody was worn to a frazzle, we went to dreamland: with visions of eating a great campfire breakfast next morning.

After a good night's sleep, everybody woke up at the same time, and   could see the eastern sky was getting brighter, which meant daylight was coming. We built a campfire in the side yard, heated Mama's pone bread we'd brought from home, burned our catfish on sticks over the fire, fried some fatback, and boiled coffee in a tin can. Nobody got foundered, but eating by lantern light in the great outdoors made it the best meal ever.

Everything had gone according to plan: with one small exception: the eastern sky was getting no brighter. We pondered a while and decided we had a small problem. "Wonder if the sun forgot to come up? What if it never came up again? How long would the oil last in the lantern? What about all them crashing noises I'd heard in the wood at night?" No way did we need to be out there in the dark in middle of nowhere with no light.

Since everybody was already wide-awake, we headed for home, knowing it would be daylight long before we walked the long road back by Bates Hill on Lambsburg Road. (That was the only way an automobile could get to Houston's house *and* the best road to be on in case we had to run from something.)

When we finally got to Bate's Hill, the sun still hadn't come up and we were tired, worried, and fresh out of ideas. Something had gone badly wrong somewhere and bad things were not supposed to happen to good guys like us.

We continued up Bate's Hill to the state line, where we met a foxhunter, (Jack Bryant) who was listening to his dogs run in the Knobs. (It was a great relief to know there were still other people alive in the world.) When we asked him what time it was, he solved all of problems with his pocket watch: it was 2:00 in the morning. That was our first and only nighttime camping trip.

Stewart's Creek continued downstream beside Houston's Bottom to a ford that crossed the creek to the Cleve Thomas place. It was a great place to wade in summer, throw rocks in the water and track honeybees back to their trees when they came to get water on the sandbars.

Mike at the Houston Hole (1971)

The Houston Hole was a few hundred feet below the ford: the fastest, deepest, darkest fishing hole on the whole creek. To get to it, you had to slide down a ten foot sandy bank and to get back up into the bottom, you had to claw and dig.

One memorable day, I almost caught my biggest trout there. When the pole bent double, I jerked the fish out of the water; it came off the hook and splashed back in. It was a terrible disaster and if the hole hadn't been so deep and fast, I would've jumped in after it. I grieved for days and fished there every chance I got: hoping it would bite again but it never did.

A jungle of rocks and blackberry briars blocked the creek bank below the Houston Hole, so everybody used a bypass path that led over a small hill to the Kettle Spring. Someone had installed an enamel kettle in the spring for a reservoir, and everybody that came by drank the "fanciest, coldest water in the whole country."

A rusty steel barrel, some rotten planks and a pile of rocks were all that remained of an ancient moonshine still near the spring. At one time, making moonshine was the only way many people had of making extra money, maybe their only money. Evidently, there were epidemics of hard times in years gone by, because I found old still places along almost all of the backwoods streams.

The Kettle spring fed into a branch that came from the springs of Oscar Marshall, Jim Smith, Farley Smith, and Sid Marshall farther up

129

the valley, then fell into Stewart's Creek at the Upper Hole. An ancient hillside pasture had gone back to the forest, and the trees that were once used for fence posts had grown until the wire was in the center of the trunks.

The Upper Hole (1971)

The road continued downstream around the hill through a tangle of honeysuckle and blackberry vines. It had been dug out of the hillside many years ago and according to my parents, it was once well traveled. (I almost never saw anyone else there when growing up.)

The "Old House" (1971)

The road continued across a spring branch and up a small grade to Oscar and Lillie Marshall's 'Old House." William Johnson's daughter Mea, married John Coalson and they built the house about 1880. Two of their sons died young and are buried in a small cemetery beside the Graveyard Road on top of the hill.

Sam Coalson lived there alone in the late 1930s, and talked about the Good Old Days. He was getting on in years, had white hair, a long white beard and frightened me out of my wits, when he told about a hole in the front door that was made by shotgun when someone tried to kill John Coalson while he lived there.

A no-longer used garden space had grown up in sassafras, blackberry briars, and locust bushes. I found some scrap lumber at an old sawmill place nearby, made toy airplanes, bobwhite traps, and whirley-gigs. (During the Big War, I whittled out a fighter plane that hangs today in the ceiling of my basement: still on watch for Japanese Zeroes.)

Oscar's Big Bottom: with Sugar Loaf Mountain in the background
(1971)

We sharecropped Oscar's two bottoms in the early years, along with three others at various times. Corn grew well in Oscar's Big Bottom with one exception: a small red-dirt slope near the house where creek rocks grew by the hundreds and more came up after every rain. (When the Big Bottom photo was made in 1971, the land hadn't been farmed for several years and had grown up in broom straw.)

The "Low Foot-log" led from the Big Bottom to the Little Bottom across the creek. It was a plain economy model: a round log with no handrail to hang on to. In summer, we just waded the creek, but it was a different story in winter. It bounced like a rubber ball when you got out in the middle and some people took an unwanted bath, sometimes in the coldest part of the year.

Honeysuckle vines covered both creek banks and we were told, "You-all stay out 'a there. They's cottonmouths, copperheads, rattlers and no tellin' what else in that mess and they don't none of 'em like nobody."

An old no-longer used road led from the backside of the Little Bottom, uphill through the woods to the Cleve Thomas home. It was the most direct way to his house, and was the way I traveled when "Mr. Cleve" bought a pack of garden seeds from me. It was in winter, and he and his wife Zelphia were warming by the fireplace in the dark room.

The Lower Hole (1971)

The Lower Hole was just downstream from the Low Foot Log: my favorite fishing hole on all of Stewart's Creek. When the "air was just right," we could hear the rapids (seen in the photo) from our house a half-mile away: singing me a fishing song.

The rapids smoothed out into the Lower Hole in a left-hand curve, where white bubbles, sticks and trash floated continually in a clockwise back-eddy against the bank. I sat in the shade of alder bushes, and watched muskrats pull green cornstalks into their dens, as buzzards circle high in the sky: searching for something dead. A big white bird Pa called a "shikepoke" (probably a crane) sometimes flew over. It looked like something was pulling it along by its head: with its neck stretched far out in front. It flapped its wings so slowly I wondered how it stayed in the sky.

On hot summer days, I sat at the Lower Hole, and hatched out some great daydreams, while waiting for the fish to bite. I found arrowheads in the bottoms and could almost see an Indian village backed up against the sunny hillside. There was nowhere else I'd rather be, but a thunderstorm or suppertime brought many great missions to an end. Hopefully, another day would come tomorrow and I'd be there: trying to catch the biggest fish the world had ever seen.

Mike and Dad resting at the Swimming Hole (1971

The Swimming Hole was some thirty feet downstream: with a house-sized rock for a diving board. Everybody went swimming in their birthday suits and anyone goofy enough to show up in a swimsuit would've been laughed out of the county. Pa and I never learned to swim, but we did some hellacious big splashing at the Swimming Hole.

One hot summer day, we decided to go for another a swim. We'd always worn our birthday suits, but something new had happened: hair was growing on me in strange places. Such things as the facts of life were never discussed in my family and rather than be embarrassed, I sneaked Pa's razor and did some shaving. We then made our last swim together.

Mama and us kids had been to Zora Thomas Harrison's home one Sunday, and while going back home, I ran on ahead and overtook two neighborhood girls who had been swimming in the Swimming Hole. They asked if I'd been down at the creek watching them swim. Of course I hadn't and they finally believed me when Mama and the others caught up with us. I thought about that quite a bit and wondered if they too went swimming in their birthday suits.

(In later years, someone told about Pa watching some girls swim at the Swimming Hole when he was growing up. I never had enough nerve to ask, but wondered if *they* went swimming in their birthday suits.)

Mike at the rainy-day shelter (1971)

A huge overhanging rock in Oscar Marshall's Bluff was my rainy-day shelter, and at some long-ago time, someone had built a campfire under it. It may have been the Indians, or maybe Daniel Boone camped there and never told anybody. I thought about camping there overnight, but I'd heard some terrible crashing noises in the woods at night, and no way was I about to camp anywhere, except in the daytime.

Pa, some other people and I went 'possum hunting one night in the nearby Cleve Thomas Woods. The smell of burning kerosene from the lantern was comforting and with other people around, I was a brave soul in the woods in the dark.

We climbed through blackberry briers, laurels, and honeysuckle vines to a tree where the dogs had treed a possum. They tried to climb the tree, until someone aimed his flashlight along his gun barrel and shot the possum. It was the only one I ever saw while possum hunting and somebody had 'possum for breakfast.

Stewart's Creek near the Woods Hole. (1971)

The Woods Hole was a few hundred feet downstream: between the Cleve Thomas and Oscar Marshall Woods, where a huge slab of rock angled into the sky. It looked like a good place to fish, but I never had any luck there.

We once found a dead white skinned animal about a foot long floating at the hole. Pa said it was a water baby and that was all I needed to know about that.

Every spring, Grandpa gathered wild herbs from under a laurel thicket at the Woods Hole and brewed up his "herb bitters." (A spring tonic to thin winter-thickened blood.) His thinking was that anything green that could stand the rigors of winter had terrific healing properties. Just like Pa's moonshine, it was guaranteed to heal any ailment known to mankind.

Pa brewed up his own version of blood thinner deep in the backwoods and when he drank a few slugs, he was a happy man. Both disasters tasted awful, but both he and Grandpa could drink the stuff straight from the jars without frowning.

A north-facing bluff to the south blocked the winter sun, which made the Woods Hole a very cold place. Grandpa told about driving his horse and wagon on the ice when the creek froze solid. I was often there in winter, but never saw the creek frozen solid. (When my son Mike and I were there in February of 1971, round icicles had frozen on twigs that hung down near the water.)

Just downstream were the bottoms of my grandfather, Cleve Thomas and Dave Carson: an area we called 'The Bottoms."

"The Bottoms" (1971)
In the foreground: George Easter's Bottom. At center, Cleve Thomas's Bottom and just beyond, Dave Carson's two small bottoms.

The George Easter Bottom (1971)

The creek idled along slow and smooth beside the George Easter bottom, where muskrats built dens in the honeysuckle banks. George was my grandfather and we sharecropped his bottom in the early years. (While hoeing corn there on the hottest days, I thought the sun would never go down.)

Mike at Grandpa's Bottom, looking toward Stewart's Creek
(1971)

The High Foot Log crossed Stewart's Creek beside a ford between Grandpa and Cleve Thomas's bottoms. It hung high in the air and was chained to poplar trees at both ends to keep it from washing away when the creek flooded. With a handrail to hang onto and planks nailed on it to walk on, it was a first class foot-log, as foot logs go: the kind to sit in the middle of on a summer day and daydream.

An August 1940 hurricane brought what became known as the "Forty Flood." It was the biggest flood ever seen on Stewart's Creek and when the water went back to normal, the foot log that never washed away *had*, along with the poplar trees, chains, planks and handrail.

My high dry road to everywhere that mattered was gone as if it had never been and I could no longer get to the Abe Hole and Dave's bottoms without wading or fighting through a tangled bluff. It was a major disaster and I think Stewart's Creek stopped running until it was replaced.

Beyond the ford, the Cleve Thomas Road led uphill by the home of Harvey Lee and Virginia Galyean Thomas, who lived in a two-room shotgun shack that had vertical plank walls and a rusty tin roof. My family and I visited while they lived there.

Just over the hill was the home of Grover Cleveland (Cleve) Thomas and his wife Zelphia. Their children were Bruce, Ellis, Violet, Tyler B, Grover, Walter, Oah, Cuban and Harvey Lee: all older than me. Their two youngest sons died in the 1940s; Cuban died in an automobile wreck on Pine Ridge Road in1942 at age 21, and Harvey Lee died in 1947 at age 24.

Four of the Thomas boys:
From the left: Cuban, Harvey Lee, Walker, and Oah, about 1940
(Courtesy of Judy Marshall Fulda.)

The Spruce Pine Hole

A small spring branch began in the Tom Hawk's Woods, and another that began in Jim's Knob met at Grandpa's house, where his spring branch and the Little Spring branch joined in. Everything then continued a half-mile down the valley and fell into Stewart's Creek at the Spruce Pine Hole: named for a tall spruce pine that stood in the hillside. It was a deep fast hole, where the creek ran against a huge rock on the south bank.

I caught my biggest trout at the Spruce Pine Hole, and thought I'd caught a whale. When it bent the fishing pole double, I yanked it out on the sandbar, and it fell off the hook. Lucky for me, the Gods smiled, and after chasing it all over the creek bank, I grabbed it just before it flopped back in the water.

It was *not* my most graceful catch, and I looked all around to see if anybody was watching. Since nobody was, I never told anybody how I landed the biggest trout of my life. It was almost as big as the one that got away at the Houston Hole.

Hundreds of water-worn creek rocks were scattered around the Spruce Pine Hole; some were waist high, and it was hard to believe floodwater could move anything that big and heavy. I panned for gold in the sandbars and fished for the suckers that swam there in winter, but like tracking rabbits in the snow, they acted like they didn't even know I was there.

A laurel Hell in the north facing bluff began downstream at the Curve Hole, and continued beyond Grandpa's house far up the valley. It was almost impossible to climb through, and my clothes got so dirty Mama threatened to dis-own me.

Stewart's Creek ran rough and rocky for the next three hundred feet beside the Cleve Thomas's Bottom. The banks were ten feet high and the rough water made it hard to stay on-foot when wading there. That didn't matter in summer, because you just got wet, but winter was a different story. Nothing under the sun got my attention like a wading boot full of icy creek water.

The creek continued downstream to Dave Carson's two little bottoms and splashed out into the "Abe" Hole: named for someone named Abe (probably Abraham) who drowned there a long time ago.

A small spring branch between the two little bottoms fell into the Abe Hole beside a white walnut tree. The walnuts had a softer shell than black walnuts and a great greasy taste. The tree leaned out over the water, where most of the walnuts fell in and washed away.

The best place to fish the Abe Hole was from a sandbar across the creek, which required wading the rough water down from the Spruce Pine Hole or climbing through the laurel bluff.

There were no deer, bears, turkeys or "painters" (panthers) in our country when I was young, and the only groundhogs lived up in the mountains. When I found some deer tracks going up the ten-foot bank at the Abe Hole, I almost fell out of my tree.

Pa's favorite fishing place was from the top of a fifteen-foot high rock below the Abe Hole. He was King of the River as he sat there fishing and smoking roll-your-own Golden Grain cigarettes, as the creek rolled by on both sides.

While fishing there one day, he did an Indian war dance when a lizard ran up inside his pants leg. He came out of his pants and almost jumped off the rock. My brother and I hee-hawd our heads off; he said, "It ain't all that damned funny."

A path led from Dave's little bottom up over a small ridge, by some huge beech trees. Through the years, people had carved their initials in the smooth beech tree bark: some so long ago, they were unreadable. Claude Marshall had carved his there, "CRM 1937" and I added mine: HWE 1940

The High Rock Hole was just below the beech trees: with a twenty-foot high rock ledge to sit on while fishing. Mayflowers grew in a small bottom across the creek, and just beyond was Gardner's hickory trees in the hillside. Pa and I killed more squirrels there than at all other places combined. (He killed the most, because his shotgun, according to him, "throwed the most lead."

The creek continued through a rapids area and fell into the sharp left-turn of the Curve Hole. Floating leaves, white bubbles, and trash circled forever in a clockwise back-eddy. Huge white pines and spruce pines stood high in the rocky bluff and black berries, raspberries and fox grapes grew on the far bank. I burned some small fish I'd caught over a smoking campfire on the Curve Hole sandbar and they were almost edible.

The creek continued into the woods toward Dave Carson's Big Bottom. There were other great fishing holes in that area, but it was getting a little far from home. The part I liked best was the two-mile stretch from the Curve Hole, back to the state line. Any time I had some free time, that was where I headed and I almost never saw anyone else in the whole area.

(I moved away in the 1950s: knowing my favorite part of Stewart's Creek would always be there when I went back: just like I left it, and so it was until.....!)

The End

Around 1970, word came of a flood control dam to be built near Dave Carson's bottoms. The lake water would back up two miles to the North Carolina-Virginia state line: covering the very bluffs, bottoms and fishing holes I knew best on my favorite part of Stewart's Creek.

On a February Sunday in 1971, my son Mike and climbed along the creek banks and made photos of some of the bottoms, fishing holes and other areas that were going under water. (With the foot logs long gone, and an icy tangled bluff blocking the way, we did not go below the Spruce Pine Hole, and I now wish we had.)

(All photos in the previous chapter (those captioned "1971) were made that day, the Line Hole photo was made in 2009, some 38 years later. The two following photos were made Easter Sunday, April 2, 1972 and the very last one was made of Watershed Lake) in 2002.

My dad on the unfinished dam
Easter Sunday, April 2, 1972

By 1972, the creek banks had already been cleared by bulldozers and the dam construction was well under way, as shown in the photo. The Cleve Thomas Bottom was just above the top of the tower and the Curve Hole was left of the tower.

The Abe Hole and Dave Carson's little bottoms were located at the extreme right center, beyond my dad. My grandfather's bottom was on the left side of the creek: (seen in the left background) about where the High Foot Log was located.

The cleared hillside at left center was once part of the mile-long laurel bluff that ended in the Tom Hawks Woods above my grandfather's house. In the far background, wind snow was falling on the Blue Ridge Mountain.

Easter Sunday, April 2, 1972
From the left: my dad, my brother Warren and our son Mike
at the dam site, Easter Sunday, April 2, 1972. The Cleve Thomas
Woods are at left center and in the far background is
Sugar Loaf Mountain at Lambsburg

One dark snowy day in March 1947, my grandfather, George Washington Easter died alone on Stewart's Creek: When he failed to come home at mid-day, Grandma went to the bottom and found him where he had died: on the creek bank beside the High Foot Log.

He was lying on his side with his arm under his head for a pillow, as he often did while taking a nap in the floor. He may have fallen in the creek and froze to death, because it was a cold day and his clothes were wet. Big snowflakes kept falling, but they soon melted and someone said, "Snow don't amount to much this time of the year."

Stewart's Creek was never again the same, because Grandma sold the home place that fall, which brought some huge changes into our lives. We could no longer use their fields, tobacco barns, and pack house, and were forced to become more independent.

142

Grandma then moved in with her daughter Maude, and lived there until she died in November, 1963

My last look at the Stewart's Creek I grew up with.
(1971)

Thanks to Watershed Lake, spring will never again come to my favorite part of Stewart's Creek: the part I grew up with, the part I knew best, and the part I liked best. Never again will corn grow in the creek bottoms: tall enough to reach the sky. Never again will anyone pan for gold in the sandbars, go skinny-dipping in the Swimming Hole, seine the Abe Hole, or sit in a certain look-out tree high in the bluff, and watch the world go by down below.

Somewhere in time and memory, all of the old fishing holes, creek banks, bluffs and bottom lands are still there, buried deep under Watershed Lake. Maybe, just maybe, when nobody is looking, when the air is just right, some moonlit night, Stewart's Creek will once again sing me a fishing song, as it falls down over the rapids at the Lower Hole and maybe, just maybe, spring will come once again to the only river I ever really knew: my river, my Stewart's Creek.

Watershed Lake at my grandfather's
home place
(2002)

Made in the USA
Middletown, DE
28 December 2023

46932591R00084